EARLY YEARS CARE
and EDUCATION

NVQ/SVQ LEVEL 3 WORKBOOK

Second Edition

MARILYN BRADBURN, DAWN REA AND KATHY WARD

Hodder & Stoughton

A MEMBER OF THE HODDER HEADLINE GROUP

Orders: please contact Bookpoint Ltd, 39 Milton Park, Abingdon, Oxon OX14 4IU. Telephone: (44) 01235 400414, Fax: (44) 01235 400454. Lines are open from 9.00–6.00, Monday to Saturday, with a 24 hour message answering service. Email address: orders@bookpoint.co.uk

British Library Cataloguing in Publication Data
A catalogue record for this title is available from The British Library

ISBN 0 340 747889

First published 1999
Impression number   10 9 8 7 6 5 4 3 2 1
Year   2005 2004 2003 2002 2001 2000 1999

Cover illustration by Jane Taylor
Typeset by Wearset, Boldon, Tyne and Wear
Printed in Great Britain for Hodder & Stoughton Educational, a division of Hodder Headline Plc, 338 Euston Road, London NW1 3BH by Redwood Books, Trowbridge, Wiltshire.

CONTENTS

ACKNOWLEDGEMENTS

The authors would like to thank John Young, Vice Principal, Administrations at Birmingham College of Food, Tourism and Creative Studies for his professional expertise and support in undertaking this venture.

INTRODUCTION

National Vocational Qualification In Early Years Care and Education Level 3 is a qualification based on standards of performance recognised by employers in the early years sector.

Because the standards relating to performance are set by the early years sector, they demonstrate that you have achieved the knowledge, skills and abilities to a satisfactory standard needed for a particular job, and are competent to work within the Early Years sector.

National Vocational Qualifications are arranged in **units** which will relate to particular areas of the job role within the early years sector. Therefore units are made up of **elements** which provide activities related to specified areas you would be employed within.

The **performance** criteria related to each area will assist you in defining what is expected to perform the activity well and demonstrate your competence. The **range statements** describe the situations that have to be covered during your assessment.

The **knowledge and understanding** relate to the specific knowledge and understanding needed to be employed within the early years sector and provides the necessary knowledge and skills needed to do the job well.

GUIDE TO TERMS

STANDARDS
Relate to the job role

UNITS
Relate tasks of the job

ELEMENTS
Relates what a person can do

PERFORMANCE CRITERIA
Relates to competent performance

RANGE
Circumstances in which the job is performed

KNOWLEDGE
Relates to what a person needs to know

EVIDENCE REQUIREMENT
Relates to how a person demonstrates competence

TO OBTAIN A NVQ/SVQ LEVEL 3 EARLY YEARS CARE & EDUCATION YOU WILL NEED
11 MANDATORY UNITS
PLUS 3 OPTIONAL UNITS

TOTAL OF 14 UNITS

GUIDE TO UNITS

MANDATORY UNITS

C2	Provide for children's physical needs.
C3	Promote the physical development of children.
C5	Promote children's social and emotional development.
C7	Provide a framework for the management of behaviour.
C10	Promote children's sensory and intellectual development.
C11	Promote children's language and communication development.
C15	Contribute to the protection of children from abuse.
C16	Observe and assess the development and behaviour of children.
E3	Plan and equip environments for children.
M7	Plan, implement and evaluate learning activities and experiences.
P2	Establish and maintain relationships with parents.

OPTIONAL UNITS

C14	Care for and promote the development of babies.
C17	Promote the care and education of children with special needs.
C18	Develop structured programmes for children with special needs.
M2	Manage admissions, finance and operating systems in care and education.
M6	Work with other professionals.
M8	Plan, implement and evaluate routines for children.
M20	Inform and implement management committee policies and procedures.
P4	Support parents in developing their parenting skills.
P5	Involve parents in group activities.
P7	Visit and support a family in their own home.
P8	Establish and maintain a child care and education service.
MCI C1	Manage yourself.
MCI C4	Create effective working relationships.
C24	Support the development of children's literacy skills.
C25	Support the development of children's mathematical skills.

MANDATORY UNITS

Unit C2	Provide for children's physical needs

C.2.1   Plan, prepare and provide food and drink for children.
C.2.2   Contribute to children's personal hygiene.
C.2.3   Respond to illness in children.
C.2.4   Plan and provide quite periods for children.

Unit C3	Promote the physical development of children

C.3.1   Develop children's confidence in movement.
C.3.2   Develop children's skills of locomotion and balance.
C.3.3   Develop children's gross motor skills.
C.3.4   Develop children's fine motor skills.

Unit C5	Promote children's social and emotional development

C.5.1   Enable children to adjust to the setting.
C.5.2   Enable children to relate to others.
C.5.3   Develop children's self-reliance and self-esteem.
C.5.4   Enable children to recognise and deal with their feelings.
C.5.5   Enable children to develop a positive self-image and identity.
C.5.6   Prepare children to move on to new settings.

Unit C7	Provide a framework for the management of behaviour

C.7.1   Negotiate and set goals and boundaries for behaviour.
C.7.2   Promote positive aspects of behaviour.
C.7.3   Respond to unwanted behaviour.

Unit C10	Promote children's sensory and intellectual development

C.10.1   Develop children's attention span and memory.
C.10.2   Develop children's awareness and understanding of sensory experiences.
C.10.3   Develop children's understanding of mathematics and science.
C.10.4   Develop children's imagination and creativity.

Unit C11	Promote children's language and communication development

C.11.1   Identify stages of children's language and communication development.
C.11.2   Provide activities, equipment and materials to extend and reinforce children's language and communication development.
C.11.3   Share books, and stories and rhymes to expand children's language and communication development.
C.11.4   Provide communication opportunities to enhance and reinforce children's language and communication development.
C.11.5   Interact with children to promote their language and communication development.

Unit C15	Contribute to the protection of children from abuse
C.15.1	Identify signs and symptoms of possible abuse.
C.15.2	Respond to a child's disclosure of abuse.
C.15.3	Inform other professionals about suspected abuse.
C.15.4	Promote children's awareness of personal safety and abuse.

Unit C16	Observe and assess the development and behaviour of children
C.16.1	Observe children's behaviour and performance.
C.16.2	Use observation results to inform the children's future care and education.

Unit E3	Plan and equip environments for children
E.3.1	Establish and maintain a safe environment for children.
E.3.2	Establish and carry out safety and emergency procedure.
E.3.3	Select furniture and equipment for children.
E.3.4	Organise and maintain the physical environment for children.

Unit M7	Plan, implement and evaluate learning activities and experiences
M.7.1	Plan a curriculum to facilitate children's learning and development.
M.7.2	Develop individual learning programmes for children.
M.7.3	Implement planned learning activities and experiences.
M.7.4	Evaluate planned learning activities and experiences.

Unit P2	Establish and maintain relationships with parents
P.2.1	Develop relationships with parents new to the setting.
P.2.2	Plan setting – in arrangements with parents.
P.2.3	Exchange information with parents about their children.
P.2.4	Share and care and management of children with their parents.

OPTIONAL UNITS

Unit C14	Care for and promote the development of babies

C.14.1	Provide for the nutritional needs of babies.
C.14.2	Manage the physical care of babies.
C.14.3	Promote the physical growth and development of babies.
C.14.4	Provide stimulation to foster the development of babies.
C.14.5	Promote the language development of babies.

Unit C17	Promote the care and education of children with special needs

C.17.1	Enable children with special needs to participate in activities.
C.17.2	Support parents to respond to the special needs of their children.
C.17.3	Contribute to the use of specialist equipment.
C.17.4	Communicate with children with special needs.
C.17.5	Contribute to the inclusion of children with special needs.

Unit C18	Develop structured programmes for children with special needs

C.18.1	Contribute to the assessment of children's developmental levels.
C.18.2	Contribute to planning structured programmes for children with special needs.
C.18.3	Implement programme activities.
C.18.4	Support parents in implementing structured programmes.
C.18.5	Contribute to the evaluation of structured programmes.

Unit M2	Manage admissions, finance and operating systems in care and education settings

M.2.1	Receive and disburse monies.
M.2.2	Implement admissions procedures.
M.2.3	Maintain operations records.
M.2.4	Operate budgets.
M.2.5	Operate systems for the supply of equipment and materials.

Unit M6	Work with other professionals

M.6.1	Develop working relationships with other professionals.
M.6.2	Share information and skills with other professionals.
M.6.3	Work in co-operation with other professionals.

Unit M8	**Plan, implement and evaluate routines for children**
M.8.1	Plan routines for children.
M.8.2	Implement planned routines.
M.8.3	Evaluate planned and implemented routines and activities.

Unit M20	**Inform and implement management committee policies and procedures**
M20.1	Prepare and present operational plans and reports to management committees.
M20.2	Implement management committee's policies and procedures.

Unit P4	**Support parents in developing their parenting skills**
P4.1	Promote parent's self-confidence in the parenting role.
P4.2	Encourage parents to relate positively to their children.
P4.3	Inform and advise parents about aspects of childcare and development.
P4.4	Help parents to develop their patterns of caring for their children.
P4.5	Support parents in their use of community support systems.

Unit P5	**Involve parents in group activities**
P5.1	Provide information and establish relationships with parents.
P5.2	Encourage parents to attend and participate in the group.
P5.3	Provide feedback to parents about their involvement in children's activities.

Unit P7	**Visit and support a family in their own home**
P7.1	Arrange to visit a family in their own home.
P7.2	Establish and develop relationships with families.
P7.3	Support families through home visiting.
P7.4	Liaise with colleagues and other professionals.

Unit P8	**Establish and maintain a childcare and education service**
P8.1	Identify and negotiate requirements for a childcare and education service.
P8.2	Establish and maintain written agreements with parents.
P8.3	Establish and maintain systems for the exchange of information with parents.

Unit MCI C1	**Manage yourself**
MCI C.1.1	Develop your own skills to improve your own performance.
MCI C.1.2	Manage your time to meet your objectives.

Unit MCI C4	**Create effective working relationships**
MCI C.4.1	Gain the trust and support of your colleagues and team members.
MCI C.4.2	Gain the trust and support of your manager.
MCI C.4.3	Minimise conflict in your team.

Unit C24	**Support the development of children's literacy skills**
C.24.1	Help develop children's reading skills.
C.24.2	Help develop children's comprehension skills.
C.24.3	Help develop children's writing skills.

Unit C25	**Support the development of children's mathematical skills**
C.25.1	Help children to use and apply mathematics.
C.25.2	Support children's understanding and use of numbers.
C.25.3	Help children develop their understanding and use of shape, space and measures.

PORTFOLIOS AND ASSESSMENT

CREATE A PORTFOLIO

Assessment for your NVQ/SVQ is based on what you can do therefore you will need to provide this evidence in the form of a portfolio. Your portfolio will be scrutinised by a wide range of people, therefore it is vital that your portfolio is well organised and that you have provided your information and evidence with an index or contents page, that sets out the sections your information are divided into. This needs to be set out in a simple form that shows your assessors how to find their way round your portfolio, directing them to your evidence quickly and efficiently. You must identify and reference every assessment.

You will need a standard A4 size folder that has divider units for each section of your work. The standards recording documentation, and your assessed work (reports, tasks, activities, etc.) At the front of your portfolio it is useful to provide your own autobiographical details in the form of a personal profile.

You need to remember that various people not only assess your portfolio associated to the award but your portfolio will also be seen by prospective employers in the Early Years Care and Education sectors.

ASSESSMENT

When you are ready to be assessed agree an appropriate assessment time with your assessor, your assessor must be a Qualified D32 assessor or a candidate assessor who is undertaking D32 training.

During an assessment your assessor will provide guidance on what areas you are competent in.

PRINCIPLES OF PROFESSIONAL PRACTICE

The Principles of Professional Practice relate to all people who are pursuing a career involved with the care and education of young children. These principles of 'Good Practice' and 'Professional Practice' are considered to set important standards that you should aspire to become and should provide a clear guideline of the expectations for professionals. A good professional is one who is working to achieve a professional qualification in the child care sector.

You need to recognise that there will be times when you will need to work in a co-operative manner with other professional staff in the care and educational sector and that by doing so you will need to understand and acknowledge the expertise and contribution made by these individuals to the benefit of young children.

You must at all times demonstrate a caring and supportive attitude to the children in your care, respect the rights of all children within society and effectively work towards promoting and supporting their rights to quality of life. It is also important to respect that each child is an individual and should be treated and respected with their individual needs in mind.

Anti-discriminatory practice should be developed and promoted in order to ensure that each child is guaranteed the same quality of service, and that positive aspects of cultural diversity are promoted.

All children should be encouraged to be as independent as possible. Children should be encouraged to make informed choices in relation to themselves and their belongings within the limits of safety.

Confidentiality of information and the source of that information should be respected at all times. Disclosure of confidential sources requires the agreement of the person concerned, therefore respecting confidential information particularly when it relates to children in your care needs careful consideration.

Professional practice requires you to understand that in the course of your involvement with children you are required to refrain at all times from disclosing such information without the consent of the child, children's parents or carers, or a person legally entitled to act on behalf of the child/children.

MANDATORY UNITS

UNIT C2 PROVIDE FOR CHILDREN'S PHYSICAL NEEDS

Descriptions of Knowledge, Understanding and Skills

Development	
1.	Basic knowledge of children's development and how provision for their physical needs affects their development.
2.	Basic dietary requirements for good health and the importance of a balanced diet and relationship of portion size and methods or preparation.
3.	The effects of illness and emotional disturbance on learning, behaviour, appetite and social interaction.
4.	Variety of food preferences, eating habits and ways these may change over time.
5.	Common food allergies.
6.	Variations of rest and sleep requirements of children at different ages and as individuals.
Curriculum Practice	
7.	The role of food in social and cultural life in shaping attitudes and behaviour.
8.	Value of introducing children to cultural and religious variations and types of food, types of preparation, utensils and eating habits.
9.	Why and how to include rest, sleep or quiet periods as part of daily routine.
10.	How to make the most effective use of space and equipment.
Equipment, Materials, Environment	
11.	Importance of attractive, easy to manage presentation of food and drink.
12.	Common dietary practices associated with religious and cultural practices.
13.	Aids available for children with special needs affecting their ability to eat independently.

Equipment, Materials, Environment – *continued*	
14.	Storage and labelling of medicines, toiletries, cleaning materials and equipment.
15.	Causes of infection and methods used to prevent cross infection.
16.	Health and safety policy and procedures of the setting and requirements.
17.	Methods of caring for personal hygiene of children, their personal hygiene requirements, including care of different types of skin and hair, and variations in family backgrounds and settings.
18.	Basic first aid required in an emergency and how to apply it, including dealing with an unconscious child.
19.	How to record and when to report incidents, significant medical conditions, administration of medicines and communicable diseases.
20.	Legal requirements in respect of parent's consent to administer medicines, creams, lotions, dressings.
21.	Symptoms of commonly encountered illnesses, and sources of help in identification and response.

UNIT C2 PROVIDE FOR CHILDREN'S PHYSICAL NEEDS

Portfolio Activities

1   Taking into account child development list basic milestones, linking in the provision for physical needs. Describe how they affect a child's development.

....

2,5,11,   Devise a booklet that would be of use to parents/carers, discussing the basic
8,12   dietary requirements and the importance of a balanced diet.

....

Include menu examples, demonstrating an understanding of cultural and religious variations, common dietary practices, sizes of portions and presentation of the food plus utensils used.

....

Suggest suitable drinks that may be offered with the meals/snacks.

....

Outline common food allergies to heighten the parents/carers knowledge and understanding.

....

This should be a detailed piece of work covering the numbered statements.

....

3   Discuss the reasons why the behaviour, learning, appetite and social interaction of a child/ren may be affected by illness and emotional disturbance.

....

4   In your workplace, research from the children their food preferences and eating habits. List these. Are there any that are not present? Suggest how these may change over a period of time.

....

7   Describe the role of food in social and cultural life in shaping attitudes and behaviour.

....

9, 10   State why and how to include rest/sleep or quiet periods as part of a daily routine. Make a plan of a room showing how you would make the most effective use of space and equipment during this time.

....

13   List the variety of aids that are available to help a child with special needs become independent whilst eating.

....

14,15,16,   Devise your own Health and Safety policy for use within the worksetting.
17,18,19,   Include all statements listed.
20,21

....

Having completed all these portfolio activities to the required standard for the level of your award, you should present your portfolio to your assessor for assessment.

UNIT C3 PROMOTE THE PHYSICAL DEVELOPMENT OF CHILDREN

Description of Knowledge and Understanding

Development	
1.	A knowledge of children's physical development and how this relates to other aspects of their development, including concentration span and how to recognise variations from developmental norms.
2.	The necessity for a gradual introduction to physical activity, building on the child's previous experience.
3.	The uses, safety factors and age appropriateness of a range of apparatus and its potential in helping children to develop gross motor skills.
4.	The contribution that the use of free creative activities make to the development of children's manipulative skills.
5.	The importance of hand-eye co-ordination and manipulative skills in the development of formal educational skills such as writing.
6.	How stereotypes about gender, racial origins or disability may affect encouragement and limit children's opportunities to participate.
Curriculum Practice	
7.	Appropriate activities and equipment that focus on developing physical control, mobility and awareness of space, and the relationship between such apparatus/activities/games and the specific physical skills to be developed.
8.	A range of strategies to encourage the participation of children in activities which will help develop motor skills, including opportunities which occur incidentally and how to use them as they occur.
9.	How to extend the children's understanding of the activities they are involved in.
10.	How to communicate verbally and non-verbally to encourage children's vocabulary about movement and spatia; awareness.

Equipment, Materials, Environment	
11.	Health and safety policy and procedures of the setting with regard to equipment, and their application in relation to the necessity for constant supervision.
12.	Appropriate indoor and outdoor activities and equipment and their potential in exploring movement with children.
13.	A range of equipment and materials for activities and games which may be used in helping children to develop gross and fine motor skills and the rationale behind their use.
14.	Adaptions to standard equipment for use by children with difficulties or special needs, and the potential use of wheeled toys, standard and adapted, for use by children with disabilities.
Relationships	
15.	How to show approval for children's efforts
16.	Range of activities that promote co-operation among children
17.	Equal opportunities policy of the setting.

UNIT C3 PROMOTE THE PHYSICAL DEVELOPMENT OF CHILDREN

3,4,5,7,8, 12,13,14 Design and make a booklet containing information on a range of apparatus that will enable children to develop and extend both their fine and gross manipulative skills. You should consider the age of the child, indoor/outdoor equipment, adaptions for children with difficulties or special needs, the importance of hand eye co-ordination and manipulative skills in the development of formal educational skills such as writing. Include reference to the contribution that the use of free creative activities make to the development of children's manipulative skills.

....

6 Prepare a leaflet for other professionals discussing how stereotypes about gender, racial origins or disability may affect encouragement and limit children's opportunities to participate. Offer them suggestions and strategies to widen participation and encourage all children to take part in physical activities.

....

11 Obtain a copy of the Health and Safety policy from your workplace. Explain how you use different apparatus safely within this policy, clearly state the level of supervision required for each piece of equipment.

....

15,16,17 Obtain a copy of the Equal Opportunities policy from your workplace. With this in mind make a list of activities that promote co-operation among children. How would you show approval for children's efforts?

....

1,2,9,10 Provide a four week plan of activities demonstrating a gradual introduction to physical activity, building on the previous experience of the children. Explain how you will extend the children's understanding of the activities they are involved in. State clearly how to communicate verbally and non-verbally to encourage children's vocabulary about movement and spatial awareness.

....

Having completed all these portfolio activities to the required standard for the level of your award, you should present your portfolio to your assessor for assessment.

UNIT C5 PROMOTE CHILDREN'S SOCIAL AND EMOTIONAL DEVELOPMENT

Description of Knowledge, Understanding and Skills

Development	
1.	Basic knowledge of children's social and emotional development and how this relates to other aspects of their development.
2.	The strategies for settling in children and the need for flexibility of approach which takes account of the developmental levels of the children, their understanding and their emotional state including the effects of separation or change and how this can affect children.
3.	How children acquire concepts of respect and care for other people and how their understanding of these concepts may change over time.
4.	The development of self-reliance and self-esteem as a gradual process and how this is affected by maturation and the development of communication skills in children.
5.	When it is appropriate to give responsibility to children, why this is important, and how family/cultural expectations of this may vary and should be handled sensitively.
6.	Stereotypical assumptions about children's self-reliance relative to gender, cultural background and disability, and how these can limit children's development.
7.	The wide range of emotions, positive and negative, covered by the 'term feelings', the powerful nature of feelings in children and aspects of control that may be appropriate.
8.	The relationship between the expression of feelings and cultural or gender stereotypes, and how such stereotypes can limit children's development.
9.	Signs of distress in a child and possible reasons for emotional outbursts and negative reactions and appropriate strategies to deal with them.
10.	Knowledge of the development of self-image and identity in children, and the additional needs regarding the development of identity which children from minority racial groups and cultures, bilingual children of mixed racial origins may have.

	Development – *continued*
11.	Difficulties which may be experienced by children with additional needs or abused children in developing a positive self-image and identity.
12.	Patterns of behaviour in children which may be symptomatic of poor self-image, and disturbed senses of identity.
13.	The importance of recognising and making use of opportunities to familiarise children with new settings.
	Curriculum Practice
14.	The range of activities and intervention strategies for maximising the potential of learning opportunities which arise in the daily routine to help children to express, discuss, control their feelings and to develop socially and emotionally.
15.	The role played by settling in objects.
16.	When to praise a child for his/her efforts and the reason behind positive reinforcement for effort.
17.	A range of strategies to encourage negotiation with children, know their possible outcomes and understand the need for flexibility in their application.
18.	How to provide activities and strategies to promote self-reliance and self-esteem and how they may be adjusted to take account of children from various cultural backgrounds, genders and with special needs.
19.	The importance for the child's social and emotional development of learning to recognise, name and deal with feelings of others and express their feelings.
20.	The planning, provision and evaluation of activities, experiences, techniques and resources which explore issues of self-image and identity in accordance with appropriate developmental levels.
21.	A variety of techniques and resources to encourage active exploration among children of different roles and identities in their play.
22.	Appropriate play activities to encourage positive expectations of the new setting and role of the carer in these activities.

Equipment, Materials, Environment	
23.	Assessment of materials and equipment which help towards the social and emotional development of children.
24.	A range of activities, routines and strategies which encourage respect for the individual child and understand the reason behind these.
25.	The importance of selecting and providing materials and resources which promote non-stereotypical views of children and adults, and which provide positive images of people who are often discriminated against.
26.	Knowledge of new settings.

UNIT C5 PROMOTE CHILDREN'S SOCIAL AND EMOTIONAL DEVELOPMENT

Portfolio Activities

1   Make a booklet about children's social and emotional development and how this relates to other aspects of their development.

....

2,13,15, 22   Devise an induction pack for new parents/carers and children. Include in the pack information on how you will help the child deal with separation and how this may affect the child. Discuss the role played by settling in objects and the range of settling in activities that you will provide and how these will encourage positive expectations of the new setting and the role of the carer in these activities.

....

3   Plan activities to be carried out over a period of time to encourage children to acquire concepts of respect and care for other people. How many children's understanding of these concepts change over time?

....

4,6,16, 18   Plan and where possible carry out activities to promote self-reliance and self-esteem for children of different ages. Suggest ways of modifying your plans to take account of children from various cultural backgrounds, genders and with special needs. Discuss how the development of self-reliance and self-esteem may be affected by maturation and the development of communication skills. When have you praised a child for his/her efforts, what is the reason for positive reinforcement? How many stereotypical assumptions about a child's self-reliance relative to gender, cultural background and disability limit children's development?

....

....

....

....

10,11,20   Plan three activities or games which will encourage children to explore issues of self-image and identity, take account of the additional needs regarding identity which children from minority racial groups and cultures, bilingual children and children of mixed racial origins may have, also children who have been abused.

....

5   Using a copy of your timetable for the week, highlight times when it would be appropriate to give responsibility to children. Discuss the importance of this and how cultural/family expectations of responsibility may vary and how you can handle this sensitively.

....

7,8,19   Plan a series of activities that will enable children to recognise, name and deal with the feelings of others and express their feelings, ensure that your activities cover the wide range of emotions both positive and negative and that they help to overcome possible cultural and gender stereotypes which can limit children's development.

....

9,17   List possible signs of distress in children, suggest possible reasons for emotional outbursts and negative reactions, suggest strategies that you may use to encourage negotiation with children and why there is a need for flexibility in their application.

....

12   List the patterns of behaviour which may be symptomatic of poor self-image, negative and disturbed senses of identity.

....

21,23,25   Prepare a leaflet which suggests a variety of techniques and resources to encourage active exploration among children of different roles and identities in their play. Suggest materials and equipment which help towards social and emotional development. Discuss the importance of selecting and providing materials and resources which promote non-stereotypical views of children and adults, and which provide positive images of people who are often discriminated against.

....

14, 24 Make a list of the range of activities and intervention strategies for maximising the potential of learning opportunities which arise in the daily routine to help children to express, discuss, control their feelings and to develop socially and emotionally and which encourage respect for the individual child and understand the reasons behind these.

....

 26 Describe the variety of settings available in your local area and the age groups they serve.

....

Having completed all these portfolio activities to the required standard for the level of your award, you should present your portfolio to your assessor for assessment.

UNIT C7 PROVIDE A FRAMEWORK FOR THE MANAGEMENT OF BEHAVIOUR

Description of Knowledge, Understanding and Skills

Development
1. Basic knowledge of children's development and how this affects their behaviour.
2. Techniques of observing and monitoring children's behaviour individually and in groups, the need to discriminate between relevant and irrelevant information in relation to behaviours needing attention and the principles of constructing a recording system for children's behaviour.
3. The limitations of children's memory and understanding and how this may affect their ability to comply with goals and boundaries for behaviour.
4. The reasons why framework for children's behaviour are necessary, the concept of socially acceptable/desirable behaviour and how this may vary across settings and cultures.
5. The basic principles of influencing behaviour, why it is important actively to promote positive aspects of behaviour and the principles of positive reinforcement.
6. Principles for selecting reward systems to be used, the factors and circumstances which may support or provoke change in usual behaviour pattern of children.
7. The concepts and behaviour signs of regression, withdrawal, attention-seeking, anti-social behaviour and self-damaging behaviour.
8. Key indicators of development and problem behaviour: emotional, physical, intellectual, social, communication.
9. The reasons why a calm and controlled manner is important and why physical punishment is not necessary, acceptable or effective.
Curriculum Practice
10. Ranges of possible sanctions appropriate for varying situations, including time out and removal from activities.

Equipment, Materials, Environment	
11.	Behaviour policy of the setting and how this is implemented.
12.	The 1989 Children Act in regard to physical punishment of children.
13.	The possible role played by additives and chemicals in food and drink.
Relationships	
14.	The central role played by parents in children's welfare and development and the bond between children and parents.
15.	How to listen and communicate with parents as equals.
16.	The rights of parents to access information held within the setting and when and how to share such information with them.
17.	Variations in family values and practices across cultural and other groupings and awareness that practices also vary within such groups.
18.	The reasons for offering explanations and discussing socially desirable behaviour with children.
19.	The importance of boundary setting and consistency of application by significant adults.
20.	The sources of specialist advice and guidance and how to gain access to them.

UNIT C7 PROVIDE A FRAMEWORK FOR THE MANAGEMENT OF BEHAVIOUR

The implementation of The Children Act 1989 investigated all aspects and forms of provision for children in order to insure that appropriate policies exist. Therefore policies that evolve from this legislation are there to protect children, the parents and the carers and all who are involved with children.

Also working in support of these **essential policies** are those policies that are considered to be important to help children develop the life skills needed to live and socialise within a community. They represent the way in which an organisation has identified a philosophy for dealing with these policies.

Behaviour Policy

A behaviour policy should be implemented as part of the workplace quality assurance. This will set out the workplace standards and guidelines on all areas of Behaviour Management. Providing information to the children, parents carers, and governors in a form that is clearly identifiable about the way behaviour is managed within the workplace.

 Portfolio Activities

To help assist you with the following activities you will need to access a copy of your workplace policy on behaviour management or an appropriate example.
As part of a staff development training day you have been asked to join the team whom are working on practice guidelines for the implementation of behaviour management policy.

11.1.3.4   Provide a brief statement that describes the aim of the policy and what it sets
8.17   out to achieve.

....

Provide six **rules** that describe and would help a child to demonstrate acceptable behaviour, and promote positive behaviour, along with setting the framework for behaviour. The rules must consider the well-being of others within the setting, and be appropriate for use by all staff. Take into consideration the developmental levels of understanding of the children they apply to.

....

18.19   At least one of these rules must take account of the workplace Equal Opportunity Policy. You need also to describe how you could modify these rules to consider socially acceptable behaviour representative of different cultures and settings within the workplace.

....

     Describe also how at 'Circle Time' you would introduce these rules to an appropriate age group as part of the concept of socially acceptable behaviour. Explain how you would verbally encourage the use of these rules with examples of how you would respond to negative behaviour.

13   Design a poster for use on the noticeboard within your workplace, that will provide parents with the information on how various additives and chemicals in some foods children eat and drink can effect behaviour.

....

Behaviour Policy

As part of behaviour policy there must also be a support system that promotes positive aspects of children's behaviour. This should include non-aggressive strategies for children to promote their rights and have the opportunity to be listened to by adults.
The opportunity to release feelings creatively along with acknowledgement that each child is an individual who will need their own time and space to understand how to achieve socially.
Acceptable behaviour will also mean that there must be sanctions and a reward system that will be consistently applied by all staff within the workplace, and in ways that is appropriate to the children's developmental level.

 5.6.14   To encourage positive aspects of behaviour devise an activity plan that takes a child centred approach.
That will enhance self-esteem while also addressing rewards, as part of a planned activity developing a child's positive behaviour, throughout the activity.

    It is important that you take into consideration the abilities and interest of the child in relation to the planned activity.

    Using the appropriate boundaries of confidentiality state the details of the child you carry the activity out with. The type of workplace and the activity setting. You need to state the aim and intended outcomes of the activity, and how it will promote positive and socially acceptable behaviour and the reward involved.

    Finally you will then carry out the activity and evaluate with reference to the physical, intellectual, social emotional and moral development, of the child, and how you could share the outcomes of this activity with the parents of the child.

....

SCENARIO

Tommy is a healthy 4-year-old who is reaching his milestones. He has had his immunisations and height and weight checks, all are normal. There has been some slowing up of weight recently but his mother states he has had a bad cold, which has resulted in his eating being picky but he likes to snack on crisps and sweets. Tommy uses few words but likes to explore and climb things. His mother has recently informed carers that there are problems with Tommy's father being violent and arguing. This has lead to Tommy's mother leaving the family home and moving into a flat near to the setting. Neither parents has ever deliberately hurt Tommy but he has had to sit out scenes of violence in which each parent threatens each other with knives, chairs or whatever comes to hand. Tommy has been involved with incidents of unwanted behaviour for the last two week's and at various times has also demonstrated directly challenging behaviour to a carer by refusing to do what he was asked to do. At story time he became aggressive refusing to sit with other children and shouted he wanted to watch television instead. One afternoon when Tommy was with a group of children painting he began to flick paint at another child, when the child began to cry Tommy ran over to the home corner of the room and hid there where a carer found Tommy curled up in a ball sucking his thumb. As a consequence of Tommy's behaviour you have arranged a meeting with Tommy's mother.

5.2
15
Describe how you will monitor Tommy's behaviour by use of The ANTECEDENT; BEHAVIOUR; CONSEQUENCE Approach. Or by use of MODIFIED ASSERTIVE DISCIPLINE. Give examples to support your explanations and explain why this process is important, plus the involvement of Tommy's mother.

....

2
Explain how you can plan to use observations as part of this process, and any other use of recording Tommy's behaviour.

....

6.10
Discuss the use of sanctions. The length of time for use of 'Time Out' in respect to the settings Behaviour Policy.
State how you will use 'Contract' with Tommy. The use of rewards in the form of a behaviour chart. Provide an example of a behaviour chart with explanation of use in both the setting and at home by the parent.

....

16.20   Explain who will have access to the information held by you relevant to Tommy's unwanted behaviour, and how confidentiality will be addressed.

....

9.12   Finally explain the Behaviour Policy of your setting in relation to physical punishment of children and the implication to the carer's if they were to use physical punishment.

....

Having completed all of the portfolio activities to the required standards for the level of your award you should present your portfolio to your assessor for assessment.

UNIT C10 PROMOTE CHILDREN'S SENSORY AND INTELLECTUAL DEVELOPMENT

Description of Knowledge, Understanding and Skills

Development	
1.	The usual sequence and process of intellectual development.
2.	How theories, practices and ideas are re-examined in the light of the interpretation of evidence.
3.	The needs and requirements of children with respect to sensory and intellectual development, how children's special needs might affect their sensory development, and how these might be met.
4.	The possible effects of environmental, physical, social, cultural and genetic factors in enhancing or impairing children's sensory development.
5.	How to provide appropriate experiences to extend memory and recall.
6.	The limitations of memory and concentration in young children, and factors affecting this.
7.	The role that attention and memory play in learning.
8.	How children respond to what they see, hear, smell, touch and feel.
9.	The particular difficulties which may affect the sensory development of children who use more than one language.
10.	How intellectual development is linked to the acquisition of mathematical and scientific concepts to solve practical problems.
11.	How children learn/acquire mathematical and scientific concepts and how their understanding of concepts may change over time.
12.	How children construct their own view of the world through using their own intellectual capacity and the nature of their environment.
13.	The role and value of self-expression, creative, fantasy and imaginative play in children's intellectual development.

Curriculum Practice

14.	The needs of individual children and the possible reasons for low concentration and attention.
15.	Why some children have difficulty or are reluctant to participate in imaginative and creative activities.
16.	A variety of appropriate experiences designed to encourage children's sensory development, develop attention and memory, their potential value and how to provide them.
17.	What sensory experiences are, their value and how to provide appropriate sensory experiences.
18.	How unexpected events and incidents can be used to promote sensory awareness and understanding, development of recall.
19.	How observation, discovery and exploratory learning can be used in developing children's understanding of the natural and physical world.
20.	The role of play in conceptual development.
21.	The types of concepts in the range such as shape, position, size and quantity.
22.	Why some concepts may be difficult for children to understand.
23.	How to provide a range of activities which involve sorting, matching, sequencing and counting.
24.	Ways to encourage children to express themselves freely and how to build on children's own interest.
25.	How children's expression can be constrained or conditioned by gender or other stereotypical roles and how to counteract this.
26.	Ways of supporting children's spontaneous imaginative play.
27.	The relative significance of process and product in children's creativity.

Equipment, Materials, Environment
28.   How to provide stimulating environments where children can express themselves freely and to encourage children's sensory development.
29.   The sorts of materials and equipment which may help children to express creativity and imagination and the rationale behind their use.
30.   How to adapt equipment and activities as necessary to make it easier for children with special needs to express their creativity and imagination.
Relationships
31.   How children learn and the ways in which adult interaction can facilitate this learning.
32.   When and how sensitive adult intervention is needed to help extend and develop children's imaginative play and awareness of the disruptive potential of such intervention.

UNIT C10 PROMOTE CHILDREN'S SENSORY AND INTELLECTUAL DEVELOPMENT

Portfolio Activities

1   Prepare a leaflet for parents/carers explaining the usual sequence and processes of intellectual and sensory development.

....

2   Research how theories, practices and ideas are re-examined in the light of interpretation of evidence.

....

5,6,7,14   Plan and carry out two activities that will extend memory and recall, in your findings discuss the limitations of memory and concentration in young children, and factors affecting this, describe the role that attention and memory play in learning. Suggest possible reasons for low concentration and attention in some children.

....

13,15,27   Plan a variety of free creative activities that will encourage all children to participate, observe children who take part and describe the relative significance of process and product in children's creativity, why do some children have difficulty or are reluctant to participate in imaginative or creative play, what do you think of the role and value of self-expression, creative, fantasy and imaginative play in children's intellectual development?

....

3,4,8,9, 16,17   Plan and carry out a range of sensory activities and observe how children respond to what they see, hear, smell, touch and feel, suggest particular difficulties which may affect the sensory development of children who use more than one language, describe your views on the value of your sensory activities. What needs and requirements of children with respect to sensory and intellectual development have you observed? Collect information on a range of special needs that children may have and suggest ways of meeting these needs. Discuss what may be the possible effects of environmental, physical, social, cultural and genetic factors in enhancing or impairing children's sensory development.

....

10,11,20, 21,22,23   Research how children's intellectual development is linked to the acquisition of mathematical and scientific concepts to solve practical problems, suggest how children learn/acquire mathematical and scientific concepts and how their understanding of concepts may change over time. Plan appropriate activities which include sorting, matching, sequencing and counting, observe children carrying out these activities, why do some children experience difficulty in understanding?

....

12   Describe how children construct their own view of the world through using their own intellectual capacity and the nature of their environment.

....

18   Suggest how you could use unexpected events and incidents throughout the day to promote sensory awareness and understanding, and development of recall.

....

19   Prepare a range of activities covering observation, discovery and exploratory learning that will develop children's understanding of the natural world, record your observations.

....

24,25,26   Draw a plan of a stimulating environment which may encourage children to express themselves freely, describe how you would encourage children to build on their own interests and how you would support spontaneous and imaginative play, suggest how children's expression can be constrained or conditioned by gender or other stereotypical roles and give your ideas on how to counteract this.

....

28,29,30   Plan a stimulating environment where children can express themselves freely and where their sensory development will be enhanced. Indicate on your plan the sorts of materials and equipment which may help children to express creativity and imagination. Suggest the rationale behind their use and how you would adapt activities and equipment to make it easier for children with special needs to express their creativity and imagination.

....

31,32   Describe how children learn and the ways in which adult interaction can facilitate this learning. Suggest when and how sensitive adult intervention is needed to help extend and develop children's imaginative play and awareness of the disruptive potential of such intervention.

....

Having completed all these portfolio activities to the required standard for the level of your award, you should present your portfolio to your assessor for assessment.

UNIT C11 PROMOTE CHILDREN'S LANGUAGE AND COMMUNICATION DEVELOPMENT

Description of Knowledge, Understanding and Skills

Development	
1.	Sequence of language and communication development in children and how this relates to other aspects of development.
2.	The needs and requirements of children when developing language and communication skills, how these might be met and factors which influence language and communication abilities development.
3.	Children's special needs which may affect the development of language and communication abilities and how sensory impairment may hinder language and communication development.
4.	Aspects of the way children think (such as egocentrism) at different ages which affect their ability to communicate effectively.
5.	The variety of ways in which children seek to communicate and how these may support or substitute for each other
6.	The varying age at in which children develop their discriminatory and stereotypical ideas.
7.	How respect for language, dialect and accent affects self-esteem and the need to value the children's community language and to provide opportunities for its development.
8.	The ways of obtaining and recording relevant information about children's communication development.
9.	The role of interest and participation in and enjoyment of spoken or written stories and rhymes in promoting children's language development.
10.	The interactive use of the four modes of language use i.e. listening, speaking, reading and writing, including the principles of active listening.
11.	Communication techniques which encourage children to communicate freely, including the role of positive feedback, encouragement and non-verbal behaviour as a means of communication and of facilitating and regulating verbal interaction.

Development – *continued*	
12.	The role of communication and self-expression in developing a child's self-esteem.
13.	Understanding a child's right not to talk on occasions.
Curriculum Practice	
14.	A variety of activities and games which give practice in, and extend, particular types of communication and speech in various different contexts and encourage the acting out of roles, including description, conversation, giving out instructions and the rationale for using them.
15.	How children use many different situations and methods of representing/reflecting their life experience, and the value of drama/role play in representing a child's experience.
16.	How to converse with children in ways which challenge stereotyping and discrimination.
17.	A variety of direct and indirect questioning techniques.
18.	Current thinking with regard to early reading and writing and their implications for those who work with children.
19.	The need to encourage and the basis for the development of pre-reading and pre-writing skills in children.
20.	The key role played by books and stories and rhymes in language development and communication and in laying the foundations of early literacy.
21.	How to make use of children's own stories and accounts of events.
Equipment, Materials, Environment	
22.	The importance of creating and maintaining a language-rich environment.
23.	How size and composition of the group, layout and other environmental factors may affect the child's expressions and communication.
24.	A variety of practical activities, materials and techniques which encourage and help children to represent their experiences and the rationale for using them.

Equipment, Materials, Environment – *continued*

25.	The importance of the ways in which representation in books, stories and rhymes can reinforce or counteract stereotypes based on gender, racial origin, cultural and religious groups and disabilities.
26.	Relevant criteria to evaluate books, stories and rhymes and examples to cover the range.
27.	The resources available in the community and how to use them including in the context of the promotion of a community language.
28.	How to use and/or make audio aids and visual aids.
29.	How to adapt/design the presentation to enable the participation of children with sensory impairment.

Relationships

30.	When and how to call on specialist advice to assist identification of communication development.
31.	The rules and boundaries of confidentiality within the setting with regard to child's communication abilities and family background.
32.	The role of the adult facilitator in helping a child to represent their experience and develop their idea, the candidate's own role in the development of language and communication skills and the roles of colleagues.
33.	The value of praise and encouragement in developing children's listening and communication skills.
34.	The importance of valuing the individual life and home experiences of children.
35.	The value of observing children's interaction before intervening.
36.	Factors which may make children shy and withdrawn in group situations and how to encourage and assist those experiencing difficulty to communicate in a group.

UNIT C11 PROMOTE CHILDREN'S LANGUAGE AND COMMUNICATION DEVELOPMENT

Portfolio Activities

1   Design a leaflet for parents/carers which charts the sequence of language and communication development in children, show how this relates to other aspects of child development.

....

2,3,5   Plan and carry out a range of activities which will meet the needs and requirements of the children in your setting with regard to language development and communication skills, evaluate your work suggesting how children's special needs may affect language and communication abilities and how sensory impairment may hinder language and communication development. Pay particular attention to the ways in which children seek to communicate.

....

6,7,12,16, 32,35   Consider the ways in which you converse with children, describe how you challenge stereotyping and discrimination and how you show respect for language, dialect and accent. State how this affects children's self-esteem and self-expression, discuss the varying age at which children develop their discriminatory and stereotypical ideas.

....

4   Devise a chart which illustrates aspects of the way children think (such as egocentrism) at different ages which affect their ability to communicate effectively.

....

8,30,31   Design a recording sheet for a child that will enable you to record information on children's communication development, use your sheet and discuss the value of recording this information. Suggest when specialist advice would be required and describe the rules of confidentiality.

....

9,10,11, 14,18,19, 20,33   Plan a series of activities over the course of a week linked to written stories, consider in your planning the interactive use of the four modes of language, listening, speaking, reading and writing, include the principles of active listening. Suggest communication techniques that you may use to encourage the children to communicate freely, and describe how you are going to give positive feedback and encouragement. Discuss the key role played by books, stories and rhymes in language development and communication and in laying the foundations of early literacy.

....

13 Describe your understanding of a child's right not to talk on occasions.

....

22,23,36 When working with young children it is important to create a language rich environment. Discuss how size and composition of groups, layout and other environmental factors may affect a child's expressions and communication.

....

25,26,28, 29 Devise a checklist that will help you to evaluate children's books, stories and rhymes with regard to counteracting stereotypes based on gender, racial origin, cultural and religious groups and disabilities. When your checklist is complete choose one of the books, stories or rhymes that you have evaluated, make and use an audio/visual aid that will appeal to the children in your setting. Describe how you may have to adapt/design the presentation to enable the participation of children with sensory impairment.

....

15,17,21 Describe how children use many different situations and methods of representing/ reflecting their life experience, discuss the value of drama/role play in representing a child's experience. Suggest a variety of direct and indirect questioning techniques that you may use to encourage children in drama/role play. How may you use children's own stories and accounts of events in this situation?

....

24,34 Make a list of a variety of practical activities, materials and techniques which encourage and help children to represent their experiences. Give a rationale for using them.

....

27 Find out about the resources available in the local community and how to use them in the context of the promotion of a community language.

....

Having completed all these portfolio activities to the required standard for the level of your award, you should present your portfolio to your assessor for assessment.

Description of Knowledge, Understanding and Skills

Development	
1.	Knowledge of children's social, emotional, physical, intellectual and behavioural development and their awareness of their body.
2.	The physical, behavioural and emotional indicators which may signify possible abuse, these should include: • physical injuries, bruises and abrasions in unusual sites or configurations compared with those likely to have been inflicted in age – appropriate physical play or other evidence of deliberately inflicted injury; • inflammation, infection and bleeding of genital area and anus, sexualised behaviour which is age-inappropriate, and other evidence of sexual activity; • poor standards of hygiene infection and infestation, weight loss or growth restriction and other physical signs of chronic neglect and failure to thrive.
3.	Characteristics and circumstances which make some children more vulnerable to abuse.
Curriculum practice	
4.	The role of routine observation and record keeping in identification of possible abuse and for evidential purposes.
5.	Confidentiality procedures of the setting.
6.	The possible influence of cultural, racial, gender or other forms of stereotyping on response to a child who attempts to disclose abuse and how to counteract this.
7.	How to evaluate and present different types of information from various sources and the importance of distinguishing between directly observed evidence, evidence from reliable sources, opinion and hearsay.
8.	Opportunities provided within daily routines and different kinds of games and equipment that can help children become aware of their bodies and to distinguish between appropriate and inappropriate touching, good and bad secrets.

Curriculum practice – *continued*	
9.	Strategies for building children's self-confidence and assertiveness.
Equipment, Materials, Environment	
10.	The external factors and constraints that make it difficult for children's rights to be promoted.
Relationships	
11.	The legislative framework and local and setting-specific procedures for child protection procedures for child protection and the candidate's own role and responsibilities within them.
12.	The rights and responsibilities of parents including their rights to be informed and consulted throughout any procedures necessary for child protection, their right to have access to information held within the setting or passed to other professionals, when and how to share such information with parents.
13.	The potential impact of disclosure of abuse on other family members.
14.	Roles and responsibilities of relevant professionals to whom referral could be made or from whom advice/involvement could be sought with regards to possible disclosure and how and when to access their help, including the social worker, health visitor, police officer, designated teacher, and NSPCC Child Protection officer (or NSPCC inspector).
15.	Key terms, the legal requirements of evidence and the implications for (a) involving an authorised professional at an early stage of disclosure (b) the importance of not pressurising the child, prompting or asking leading questions.
16.	Ways of listening to and communicating with children of different ages including indicators of readiness to communicate and how to deal with the aftermath including appropriate sources of personal support.
17.	The personal and emotional impact of child abuse, how to manage a controlled response to distressing disclosures and how to deal with the aftermath including appropriate sources of personal support.

Relationships – *continued*	
18.	The importance of reassurance and continued unconditional acceptance for the child in counteracting the potentially damaging effects of abuse and disclosure on self-image and self-esteem.
19.	The professional groups most likely to want information and the purposes for which this information is likely to be required including the role of case conferences and court proceedings.
20.	How to confidently and assertively pass on relevant, accurate and up-to-date information and express concerns to other professionals.
21.	The concept of children's rights and the importance of empowering children to exercise those rights.

UNIT C15 CONTRIBUTE TO THE PROTECTION OF CHILDREN FROM ABUSE

Portfolio Activities

1.8
9.10
21.3

Plan two appropriate activities that can be used with children in relation to issues of personal safety. These activities will need to provide strategies that help a child to be assertive about stating their own rights, choices, and wishes. They also need to encourage self-confidence and assertiveness.

State the age of the children you would use for each activity. Describe the setting in which each activity would take place. Your aims for each activity along with the learning outcomes for the children in relation to their social, emotional, physical, intellectual and moral development.

....

20

Describe how you would respond with appropriate reassurances to the child who gets upset at being involved with these activities. Also whom you would share this information with.

....

6

State how you would account for variations in family values and practice and how this could influence stereotypical assumptions in relation to culture, racial or gender behaviour.

....

11.12
5.13
14.4
19

Referring to a copy of your organisation's Child Protection Policy, assume you have been observing a child closely for a period of time, in relation to suspected abuse. You still feel concerned and feel the need to express your concerns further.

Discuss your role and responsibilities in relation to your settings Child Protection Policy.

State how you interpret your role relating to the legislative procedures.

What rights you feel parents/guardians have in relation to your concerns.

....

Explain how you would address confidentiality in relation to your settings policy and procedures.

....

Describe the stages you feel relevant professionals would be involved if your suspicions are founded, and the types of information that would be required by each professional.

....

Identifying Abuse

All carers working with children need to be able to identify the physical, behavioural and emotional indictors along with chronic neglect and failure to thrive, which can contribute to the possible identification of suspected child abuse. Similarly all carers need us to recognise methods of recording, observing and record-keeping for evidential purposes and legal proceedings.

2.15   Using the diagrams below record the locations of signs of
16.17   deliberately inflicted injuries that can occur in both physical and sexual abuse.

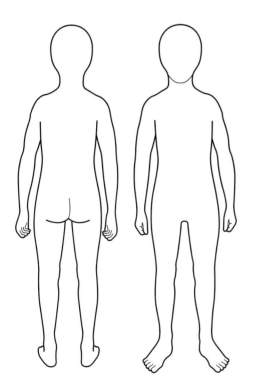

18   Describe the signs and associated symptoms you would expect to see and behavioural problems that can be associated to these.

....

Provide a range of examples of the type of routine observations that would relate to behavioural difficulties associated with suspected abuse. Record keeping that could be used for evidential purposes, and that would substantiate abuse.

....

Describe what you would associate to signs and symptoms of chronic neglect and failure to thrive. How could these be associated to child abuse?

....

Explain the type of evidence you feel you could be asked to provide in relation to directly observed evidence, evidence that is from a reliable source, and evidence that would be opinion and hearsay.

....

Describe with examples what you would consider to be an 'overt' and 'covert' message in relation to child abuse.

....

Being involved with any form of child abuse can be a distressing experience. State how you feel you would manage to respond both personally and professionally when working with a child who has been a victim of abuse?

....

Having completed all of these portfolio activities to the required standard for the level of your award, you should present your portfolio to your assessor for assessment.

UNIT C16 OBSERVE AND ASSESS THE DEVELOPMENT AND BEHAVIOUR OF CHILDREN

Description of Knowledge, Understanding and Skills

Development	
1.	Detailed knowledge of the course of all aspects of children's development, and the range of behaviours which might be expected at different ages and stages of development.
2.	Reasons for observing children's performance and behaviour on specific tasks and activities in comparison to that which is contrived for the purpose of assessment.
3.	How and why children's behaviour and performance may vary across assessment situations.
4.	Cultural, social and gender based influences on children's spontaneous and natural performance.
5.	Why repeated observations are necessary including links between concentration, performance and distractibility.
6.	How to relate examples of observed and assessed behaviour to widely accepted norms of behaviour.
Curriculum Practice	
7.	The importance of tasks, context and role of observers in some formal assessment situations.
8.	How to select tasks and activities and appropriate recording formats to meet the agreed observation objectives.
9.	How to select and use appropriate methods for observing and recording different aspects of children's spontaneous or natural behaviour.
10.	Concepts of reliability, validity and subjectivity.
11.	How and why to record features of the context and off-task behaviours when making observations of children's performance and behaviour on specific tasks and activities.

Curriculum Practice – *continued*

12.	How to summarise, interpret and evaluate data from observations and assessments.
13.	How to use observations for the purposes of the assessment and the limitations of such uses.
14.	How to use observations for developing future curriculum plans.

Equipment, Materials, Environment

15.	The uses of technology in presenting tasks and stimuli, carrying out and recording observations of children's spontaneous and naturally occurring behaviour and performance.
16.	Sources of distractions/disruptions during observation of task performance and how to minimise these.

Relationships

17.	How to communicate instructions and requests to children of different ages and characteristics.
18.	Various roles observers might play in enabling children to demonstrate their full potential.
19.	Possible cultural, social and gender based influences on children's responses to structured assessment situations.
20.	The need for parental involvement and approval in observation and assessment and the contributions that parents can make from their extensive knowledge of their own child.
21.	The rights of children when being observed and the responsibilities of adults for others in the setting.
22.	The importance of liaising with other professionals when assessing children's behaviour, abilities and development.

UNIT C16 OBSERVE AND ASSESS THE DEVELOPMENT AND BEHAVIOUR OF CHILDREN

It is anticipated that you will need around twenty detailed observations in order to be assessed as competent in this unit. You will need to liaise with your assessor often and have your observations assessed as you progress through your qualification, you will need your assessors feedback to enable you to improve your technique and increase your knowledge of children's development.

Each observation should include the following information: date and time of the observation, child's first name ONLY, date of birth, description of context, ethnicity, number of adults present, number of children present, purpose of observation and a signature and date from the person who has given you permission to do the observation. All observations should be evaluated with reference to physical, intellectual, emotional and social development unless otherwise stated. You should include a section on what you think you have learned from carrying out each observation, remember to reference your work correctly.

Portfolio Activities

1,2,3,4,5, 6,10,12, 20   Carry out general development observations of five to ten minutes duration, evaluate your observations suggesting how cultural, social and gender based influences may have affected the children's spontaneous and natural behaviour. Give reasons why you would need to repeat observations on the same child. Explain why children's performance may vary across assessment situations and suggest why you might need to observe performance and behaviour on set tasks.

....

8,11,7.15   Select a task using technology for a child to complete, design an appropriate recording format to meet the objectives of your observation. Carry out the observation and evaluate how successful your ideas were. Include reference to off task behaviour.

....

9,13,14, 20,22   Carry out a pre-reading or pre-writing observation. Design a recording format that will enable you to collect and record information yourself, other professionals and parents/carers. Use the information you have gathered about the child to generate a curriculum plan which will enable the child to develop their skills further.

....

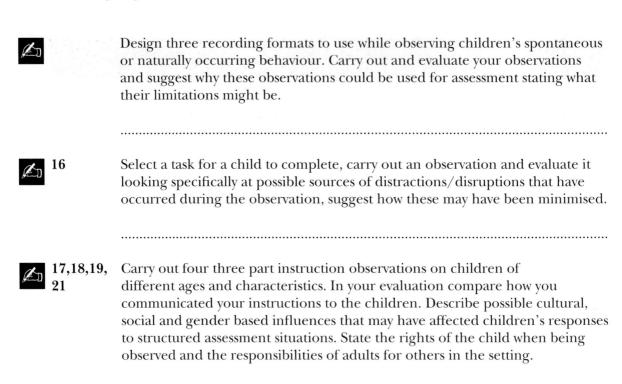

Design three recording formats to use while observing children's spontaneous or naturally occurring behaviour. Carry out and evaluate your observations and suggest why these observations could be used for assessment stating what their limitations might be.

....

16 Select a task for a child to complete, carry out an observation and evaluate it looking specifically at possible sources of distractions/disruptions that have occurred during the observation, suggest how these may have been minimised.

....

17,18,19, 21 Carry out four three part instruction observations on children of different ages and characteristics. In your evaluation compare how you communicated your instructions to the children. Describe possible cultural, social and gender based influences that may have affected children's responses to structured assessment situations. State the rights of the child when being observed and the responsibilities of adults for others in the setting.

....

Having completed all these portfolio activities to the required standard for the level of your award, you should present your portfolio to your assessor for assessment.

UNIT E3 PLAN AND EQUIP ENVIRONMENTS FOR CHILDREN

Description of Knowledge, Understanding and Skills

Development	
1.	Basic knowledge of children's development and the importance of taking account of this when considering safety arrangements and choosing furniture, fixtures, equipment and materials.
2.	Children's need to explore their environment in safety and security.
3.	How to recognise and cope with children's emotional reactions to accidents and emergencies.
Equipment, Materials, Environment	
4.	The requirements of the relevant statutory authority and any other guidance for health, hygiene and safety and supervision in the setting, including access to premises.
5.	Suitable contents of first aid box for care/education settings and the importance of checking contents on a regular basis.
6.	The health and safety hazards posed by animals in the care/education setting.
7.	Procedures for different emergencies, how to select and display those appropriate for the setting to ensure other adults are aware of them.
8.	The need to rehearse, review and modify procedures regularly.
9.	Basic first aid in an emergency, how and when to apply it, when to call professional assistance.
10.	The policies and procedures of the setting for handling and disposing of body fluids and waste material particularly in light of HIV/AIDS and hepatitis etc.
11.	Equipment suitable for children's activities at different stages to cover all areas of development.

Equipment, Materials, Environment – *continued*

12.	Sources of equipment and advice including any specialist equipment related to individual children's needs.
13.	How to adapt or modify furniture, equipment and the environment in response to children's special needs.
14.	Methods of stock control.
15.	Layout of furniture that can encourage and discourage different kinds of activities.
16.	Presentation of equipment and resources that can encourage/discourage different kinds of activities, including individual and group work.

Relationships

17.	Adult/children ratio specified by current statutory and non-statutory requirements.
18.	The importance of adults in the setting being aware of emergency procedures and their roles in them.
19.	How to convey information to parents without causing undue alarm.

UNIT E3 PLAN AND EQUIP ENVIRONMENTS FOR CHILDREN

Portfolio Activities

1,2,11, 13,15,16	Using your knowledge of child development, plan a safe environment for children. Consider safety arrangements, furniture, equipment and materials. State how you would adapt the environment in response to a child's special needs.

....

3 List possible signs of children's emotional reactions to accidents and emergencies. Suggest ways in which you would cope with these. These may possibly occur within or outside the setting.

....

4,17 Research your settings published guidelines on health, hygiene, safety and supervision, including access to premises. Include notes on these.

....

5,6,8,9, 10,18 Cross-referencing with unit C2, check that you have included the listed numbered statements in with your Health and Safety booklet.

....

7,19 Design your own display cards for use within your setting on three emergency procedures to promote awareness amongst other adults. Consider how to convey this type of information to parents, and carers without causing undue alarm.

....

12 Research the sources of equipment and advice available, including any specialised equipment to aid and meet a child's individual needs.

....

14 Devise or include already established documentation on monitoring stock control.

....

Having completed all these portfolio activities to the required standard for the level of your award, you should present your portfolio to your assessor for assessment.

UNIT M7 PLAN, IMPLEMENT AND EVALUATE LEARNING ACTIVITIES AND EXPERIENCES

Description of Knowledge, Understanding and Skills

Development	
1.	Detailed knowledge of the course of children's physical, social and emotional, sensory and intellectual development and language and communication skills.
2.	How to evaluate and match activities to needs and developmental level for the individual child or group.
3.	Stereotypical assumptions based on gender, racial origins or disability made in assessing children's development level and how to avoid them.
4.	The background and previous experience of the children in the group.
5.	Periods of time for which children at various stages of development are able to concentrate.
Curriculum Practice	
6.	How to develop, implement and evaluate long term plans that cover all major curriculum areas.
7.	How to develop, implement and plan medium term plans that ensure children can progress from one stage to the next within a given curriculum area, flexible enough to meet the needs of individual groups of children.
8.	How to develop, implement and plan short term plans that provide for individual needs and interests of a specific group of children, reflecting what each child is interested in, knows needs and how each child learns.
9.	The need to plan activities which reflect the social and cultural background of the children and which promote equality of opportunities for each child, including the use of festivals and special events from a range of cultures.
10.	The relevance and value of individual and group activities in promoting children's learning and development.

Curriculum Practice – *continued*	
11.	How to use assessments of development/abilities/behaviour to help develop curriculum plans and individualised learning programmes.
12.	What counts as significant evidence from observations and the concepts of validity and reliability and factors which affect this.
13.	Methods of establishing aims, objectives and learning outcomes.
14.	Why it is sometimes necessary to treat children differently or whether to treat each with equal concern.
15.	When and how to adapt or modify planned activities in a flexible way to suit children's needs and interests, capitalising on unplanned learning opportunities, making best of existing resources and ensuring the curriculum does not contain bias.
16.	How and when to provide activities which are calming and soothing.
17.	How to use own time and the children's time effectively, including when to involve children in planning.
18.	How to set and use criteria for evaluation.
19.	Methods of self-evaluation.
20.	How to evaluate curriculum plans for individual children and use the information in future planning with other members of the team.

UNIT M7 PLAN, IMPLEMENT AND EVALUATE LEARNING ACTIVITIES AND EXPERIENCES

Portfolio Activities

1,4,5,6,7, Include long, medium and short term planning. For each one write a detailed
8,9,10,13, analysis to cover the numbered statements.
15,16,17

If there is no long or medium term planning, then suggest why it may be important to implement them within your setting.

You should demonstrate an in-depth knowledge and understanding of the curriculum planning and how it meets each child's needs.

....

2,11 Devise 3 assessment activities on

- Development
- Learning ability
- Behaviour

Implement these on a small group of children of mixed abilities. From your evaluation of the completed assessments, how can you use the information to aid curriculum planning and individualised learning programmes?

....

3 Suggest possible stereotypical assumptions that maybe made on the basis of gender, race and disability when assessing children's developmental level. How can you avoid these?

....

12 Discuss what counts as significant evidence from observations made, and the concept of validity and reliability and factors which may affect this.

....

14 State why it may be necessary to treat children differently or with equal concern.

....

18,19,20 Cross-reference with M8.

Having completed all of these portfolio activities to the required standard for the level of your award you should present your portfolio to your assessor for assessment.

UNIT P2 ESTABLISH AND MAINTAIN RELATIONSHIPS WITH PARENTS

Description of Knowledge, Understanding and Skills

Development	
1.	How children at different stages and ages are likely to react to separation from parents and transition from one type of setting to another.
2.	Differing theories about settling-in and separation from parents and their implications for practice.
Equipment, Materials, Environment	
3.	Health and safety procedures with regard to different types of emergencies including accidents, emergency closure of the setting etc. and when and how to contact parents.
Relationships	
4.	The significance of the bond between parents and their children.
5.	The types of information needed by and from parents and how to exchange it, record it and keep it up-to-date.
6.	The significance of the central role played by parents in their children's welfare and development.
7.	The concept and implications of shared care and partnership with parents
8.	The policy of the setting concerning confidentiality of information.
9.	Parents rights under the relevant legislation.
10.	How to communicate with parents as equals, how to listen to parents and how to adjust and modify communication with parents, sensitively and flexibly according to their interest, knowledge and confidence.
11.	Sources of additional help and information to support developing relationships with parents, including those who experience communication difficulties.

	Relationships – *continued*
12.	The importance of using correct names and modes of address in showing respect for individuals.
13.	The apprehension some parents may feel when new to the setting and how they might show their anxieties about leaving their child with someone else.
14.	The arrangements for settling-in and how to communicate these to parents.
15.	The difficulties which may be faced by children and parents whose cultural and language background is different from the predominant culture and language of the setting.
16.	Key areas on which clear policies and mutual agreement should be established e.g. routines, boundary setting, emergencies and why exchange of information is beneficial to parents, carer and child.
17.	How pressures of parent's circumstances can affect their communication and relationships with their children and with other adults.
18.	Variations in family values and practices across cultural and other groupings and awareness that practices also vary within such groups and how to establish relationships with all parents.
19.	The candidate's role and responsibilities with regard to establishing and maintain relationships with parents and circumstances in which parents should be referred to senior colleagues or other professionals.

UNIT P2 ESTABLISH AND MAINTAIN RELATIONSHIPS WITH PARENTS

 Portfolio Activity

SCENARIO

As Senior Nursery Nurse you receive a telephone call from an anxious parent. The parent informs you that the family's personal circumstances have changed resulting in the family moving to this area. The parent informs you that they are shortly returning to full time employment. Anxiously the parent states that there will be no one to look after the youngest child who is four-years-old, and described by the parent as 'shy and needs a lot of attention'. The parents voice changes 'Would you have a place for my child? Oh and would I have to pay? If so how much will it cost for a full time place?'

---

 17   Describe how you would communicate to the parent in a reassuring manner. Explain how. In order to respond effectively to both the parent and child's needs you would encourage a follow up visit at the family home. Briefly explain the purpose of the visit to the parent; conclude by confirming the agreed appointment in a letter with accompanying brochure of the nursery.

....

 16.15   Produce a comprehensive brochure that will provide the necessary detailed
12   information and that can be clearly understood by all parents.

....

 18   State how you could modify the brochure to accommodate those parents whose cultural and language background are different from the predominant cultural and language of the setting.

....

You must include all of the following areas in the brochure:

 5.3.8   Provide an introduction in the form of a welcome letter explaining the purpose of the brochure. Also a statement that includes the ethos or philosophy of the organisation. The Mission statement of the organisation, Admissions Policy & Procedures, Equal Opportunities Policy, Health & Safety Procedures, Parents as Partners Policies, Child Protection Policies and Procedures.

....

1,2.13
14.4   Settling in Policy and Procedures.

....

19.9.10
11.7.6   Parental Involvement Policy.

....

Having completed all of these portfolio activities to the required standard for the level of your award, you should present your portfolio to your assessor for assessment.

OPTIONAL UNITS

UNIT C14 CARE FOR AND PROMOTE THE DEVELOPMENT OF BABIES

Description of Knowledge, Understanding and Skills

Development	
1.	A knowledge of the growth and development of babies up to 12 months and how this can be affected by the social, emotional and physical environment.
2.	The sequence and development of language and communication skills in babies and factors which influence learning and development, including the importance of stimulation and interaction with adults.
3.	The general nutritional requirements of babies at different ages and what constitutes a balanced diet, knowledge of dietary requirements including those associated with religious and cultural practices.
4.	The process of weaning and factors which influence it.
5.	The common food allergies and feeding difficulties and where to get advice about them.
6.	Why it is important to maintain a comfortable and relaxed atmosphere and its effects on the baby's interest and their enjoyment of food.
7.	The variation in sleep patterns in babies over time and across individuals, the importance of rest/sleep or quiet periods as part of the daily routine, of matching the routines of the home and child care setting, recognising when a baby needs sleep/rest and how to provide for it.
8.	Unusual conditions and symptoms of common ailments which may require to be reported.
9.	The needs and requirements of babies of different ages with respect to physical growth and development and how these needs might be met.
10.	The links between physical play and experiences and intellectual development.

Curriculum Practice

11.	The general role of exercise and physical play in promoting physical growth and development and how exercise and physical play can be incorporated into physical routines.
12.	The importance of turn-taking and conversational exchange.
13.	Methods of encouraging attentive listening and sound discrimination in babies of different ages.
14.	The wider function of feeding as a sensory experience and how early experiences of feeding can shape attitudes to food.
15.	A range of activities to stimulate sensory and physical development.
16.	Why it is necessary to keep records of feeds and feeding routines.

Equipment, Materials, Understanding And Skills

17.	Health, safety and hygiene requirements which should be maintained when working with babies, especially when feeding babies.
18.	Methods of food and drink preparation, presentation and preservation and hygiene and safety requirements associated with these.
19.	How to provide a suitable environment to promote stimulation.
20.	Suitable safety equipment for use with babies of different sizes and ages up to 12 months.
21.	Awareness of the effect of changes in temperature and babies' sensitivity to changes in temperature and the need to adapt the environment and clothing accordingly.
22.	Suitable toys, equipment, games, books, rhymes, stories, and songs for babies to support the development of language.
23.	Advantages and disadvantages of breast and bottle feeding, alternative types of milk which may complement breast milk and methods of storing expressed milk.

Relationships	
24.	The emotional issues around toilet training and when and how to introduce it.
25.	The importance of working in partnership with parents.

UNIT C14 CARE FOR AND PROMOTE THE DEVELOPMENT OF BABIES

Portfolio Activities

1,2,11,12   Devise and make a leaflet for parents/carers explaining in detail growth and development and the sequence and development of language in babies up to twelve months. Remember to include information on the social and emotional factors which may affect babies development. Suggest to parents/carers routines and strategies that they could use at home to encourage these areas of development.

....

3,4,5,6, 14,17,18   Produce a poster which may be used in the baby room or local health centre giving information on the nutritional requirements of babies up to twelve months include those associated with religious and cultural practices. Give information on the weaning process. Include the wider function of feeding as a sensory experience and describe how early experiences of feeding can shape attitudes to food. Highlight safety and hygiene as well as methods of food and drink presentation. Also include advice on maintaining a relaxed atmosphere while feeding and possible effects if the baby becomes distressed or disinterested.

....

9,10,13, 15,19,22   Collect together a wide range of information on equipment produced for babies which may encourage development in all areas of physical, intellectual, emotional and social development. From the information that you have gathered select two pieces of equipment for each area of development and discuss in detail why you would use this equipment in the baby room.

....

7   Observe babies of different ages over a period of one week looking at their sleep/rest patterns. Devise a daily routine that allows for both rest and sleep periods throughout the day.

....

8   Prepare a list of unusual conditions and symptoms of common ailments which may require reporting. State the method of reporting in your workplace.

....

16   Devise a record keeping system for feeding in the baby room. Over the period of a week complete your record suggesting why it is necessary to keep records such as this.

....

21   State what the average temperature should be in the baby room, why is it essential to monitor the temperature and adjust babies clothing accordingly?

....

20   Prepare a leaflet for parents/carers giving information on safety equipment for use with babies of different sizes and ages up to twelve months.

....

23   Collect together information on the advantages and disadvantages of breast and bottle feeding. Include information on how to store expressed milk and alternative types of milk which may complement breast milk.

....

24   Design a poster which could be used in your workplace giving information on potty training, suggest how and when it should be introduced and ways of dealing with the emotional issues that may occur.

....

25   State why it is important to work in partnership with parents.

....

Having completed all these portfolio activities to the required standard for the level of your award, you should present your portfolio to your assessor for assessment.

UNIT C17 PROMOTE THE CARE AND EDUCATION OF CHILDREN WITH SPECIAL NEEDS

Description of Knowledge, Understanding and Skills

Development	
1.	The overall course of children's development.
2.	Awareness of the implication of physical, intellectual and sensory disability and learning difficulties and how these affect the development of children.
3.	The range of activities and their potential in terms of child development.
4.	How to select goals linked to activities and individual progress.
5.	The individual child's need for support and independence.
6.	The links between effort, failure and achievement and self-confidence and self-esteem and methods of encouragement and support.
7.	Sequence of development of language and communication in children.
8.	How different disabilities might hinder communication.
Curriculum Practice	
9.	How to select and plan appropriate activities.
10.	How to keep records on a child's participation in activities.
Equipment, Materials, Environment	
11.	Legislation and local policies concerning inclusion in education and care provision of children with special needs.
12.	Background knowledge of the range of provisions within which children with special needs are likely to be included.
13.	A broad background knowledge of the range of specialist equipment commonly used by children with different types of special needs.

Equipment, Materials, Environment – *continued*

14.	Where and how to obtain information and skills related to availability of equipment and its use.
15.	The policies and procedures of the setting for the supply, use, maintenance and disposal of specialist equipment.
16.	How and when specific equipment should be used by the children in the setting and the reasons for their use.
17.	The policies and procedures of the agency with regard to inclusion and health and safety.
18.	Awareness of the range of systems of communication and the validity of sign systems.
19.	Where to obtain information and advice on the range and use of communication aids for visually and hearing impaired.
20.	Where to obtain support for interpretation of various home languages as relevant to the local community.
21.	The social, environmental and cultural context in which local families live.
22.	Awareness of current medical, educational and technical terminology associated with different types of special needs and where to obtain further information.

Relationships

23.	The central role played by parents in their children's welfare and development and the bond between children and parents.
24.	The types of information and skills needed by parents, how to communicate with parents as equals, how to listen to parents and how to adjust and modify communication with parents according to their interest, knowledge and confidence.
25.	The importance and value of parents' knowledge and expertise concerning their children.

Relationships – *continued*	
26.	The candidates' role and responsibilities with regard to parents and the circumstances in which parents should be referred to senior colleagues or other professionals.
27.	Variations in family values and practices across cultural and other groupings and awareness that practices also vary within such groupings.
28.	The strong emotions felt by parents about their children with special needs and how to respond with sensitivity to expressions of such feelings.
29.	How to help children to contribute to the management of their own aids.
30.	Strategies for assisting parents in helping children with special equipment.
31.	How to maintain privacy and dignity for the child.
32.	Support networks for families with children with special needs.

UNIT C17 PROMOTE THE CARE AND EDUCATION OF CHILDREN WITH SPECIAL NEEDS

Portfolio Activities

9,10   Devise a checklist for one child for a week, to keep a track of all the activities that the child participates in. Examine this record closely, select and plan appropriate activities to encourage this child's development.

....

11,12,13,   Compile a fact sheet for parents/carers and other professionals. It should include information on legislation and policies concerning inclusion in education and care provision of children with special needs. The range of provisions within which children with special needs are likely to be included.

....

14,19   Give a description of the range of specialist equipment commonly used by children with different types of special needs, the availability of it and its use. Where to obtain information on and advice on the range and use of communication aids for visually and hearing impaired children.

....

15   Obtain copies of your workspace policies and procedures for the supply, use, maintenance and disposal of specialist equipment and the policies and procedures of the agency with regard to inclusion and health and safety. State how you have implemented them in your work place.

....

20,21,27   Describe the social, environmental and cultural context in which local families live. Where could you obtain support for interpretation of various home languages as relevant to the local community, and describe how variations in family values and practices across cultural and other groupings may differ.

....

22   Collate information on current medical, educational and technical terminology associated with different types of special needs and where to obtain further information.

....

30,32   Produce a fact sheet for parents which includes information on support networks for families with children with special needs. Suggest strategies for assisting parents in helping children with specialist equipment.

....

7,8,18   Produce an information sheet for parents/carers giving detailed information on the sequence of development of language and communication in children. Include in your sheet, information on the range of systems of communication and the validity of sign systems. Give information on how different disabilities might hinder communication.

....

17   Obtain a copy of your workplace policies with regard to inclusion and health and safety. State how you implement this.

....

16,29   Make a list of the specific equipment and aids that the children in your workplace use, what are the reasons for their use? How do you encourage children to contribute to the management of their own aids?

....

23,24,25, 26,28   Produce an information/induction pack for parents/carers who have a child starting at your workplace. It should include information on the strong emotions felt by parents about their children with special needs and how your workplace deals with this issue. The central role played by parents in their children's welfare and development and the bond between children and parents. How you are going to pass information to parents and keep channels of communication open. You will need to explain to parents how you value their expertise concerning their children and how and why parents may be referred to senior colleagues or other professionals.

....

31   Design a poster for your workplace giving suggestions on how to maintain privacy and dignity for children.

....

1,2   Produce a booklet charting the overall course of children's development, include in your booklet information showing your awareness of the implication of physical, intellectual and sensory disability and learning difficulties and how these affect the development of children.

....

3,4,5,6   Observe a child in your workplace over a period of one week. Suggest a range of activities and their potential in encouraging this child's development, monitor their progress on specific activities and goals you have set. You will need to consider the links between effort, failure and achievement and self-confidence and self-esteem and methods of encouragement and support.

....

Having completed all these portfolio activities to the required standard for the level of your award, you should present your portfolio to your assessor for assessment.

UNIT C18 DEVELOP STRUCTURED PROGRAMMES FOR CHILDREN WITH SPECIAL NEEDS

Description of Knowledge, Understanding and Skills

Development	
1.	Overall course of children's development.
2.	How to observe children closely to help identify levels of development.
3.	Stereotypical assumptions often made in assessing children's developmental level and how to avoid them.
4.	The need for adaptive response to the child's behaviour.
5.	A child's need for independence, control, challenge and sense of achievement.
Curriculum Practice	
6.	Methods of establishing clear descriptions of what is to be achieved through planned activities and experiences and ways of identifying and measuring steps of achievement towards those aims and objectives.
7.	How to provide a structured activity within a group setting.
8.	The need for responsiveness and flexibility in implementation.
9.	Techniques for positive reinforcement, how it should be used and its effects on the parents and children.
Equipment, Materials, Environment	
10.	The policy and rules of the organisation and setting in regard to health, safety, observation, assessment, record keeping and confidentiality of records.
11.	Range of equipment and materials for children with special needs.
12.	Activities and strategies which are enjoyable for the child and carer whilst repeating necessary exercises.

	Equipment, Materials, Environment – *continued*
13.	The purpose of evaluation and how to use information in future planning.
14.	Methods of self-evaluation.
15.	A variety of methods and formats of planning, monitoring, observing and recording for evaluation purposes.
16.	How to collect and analyse information on children's development and family background.

	Relationships
17.	The need for parental involvement and approval in observation and assessment, the contributions that parents can make from their extensive knowledge of their own child and the value of this knowledge and expertise.
18.	The roles of other professionals in regard to observation and assessments with particular reference to co-operation in assessment, confidentiality issues and the practicalities for the candidate's setting and role.
19.	The central role played by parents in their children's welfare and development and the bond between children and parents.
20.	How to communicate with parents as equals, how to listen to parents and how to adjust and modify communication with parents according to their interest, knowledge and confidence.
21.	The importance of valuing a child and communicating this.
22.	When it is appropriate to intervene in a child's activity.
23.	The importance of responding to interacting with the child including communicating plans and intentions to the child in an appropriate way.
24.	Methods of facilitating the learning of adults.
25.	The nature of relationships within families and the importance of encouraging other family members to be actively involved with and accepting of a child with special needs.
26.	The constraints which living conditions may impose on parent's ability to sustain a programme.

UNIT C18 DEVELOP STRUCTURED PROGRAMMES FOR CHILDREN WITH SPECIAL NEEDS

Portfolio Activities

2,3,10,13, 15,16,17, 18

Design three different recording formats that you might use when observing children in your setting, carry out observations using your designs and evaluate the observations looking at physical, intellectual, emotional and social development. Discuss how your recording formats and evaluations have helped you clearly identify levels of development whilst avoiding making stereotypical assumptions which can often be made when assessing developmental level. In each observation state how you will use the evaluation in future planning. Discuss how you were able to collect and analyse information on the children's family backgrounds. Include your ideas on the importance of obtaining information from both parents and other professionals. Include in your observations a copy of your workplace policy on health, safety, observation, assessment, record keeping and confidentiality of records.

....

6,7,8,9

Include a copy of your timetable/duty rota for the week, highlight the times that you are going to provide a structured activities within the group setting. State how you have planned and implemented these activities and how you have recorded the outcomes. How have you demonstrated your flexibility and what methods have you used for positive reinforcement?

....

1

Devise a booklet for parents/carers charting the overall course of children's physical, intellectual, emotional and social development.

....

4,5,9,12, 21,23

Explore techniques that you may use for positive reinforcement, describe how it should be used and its effects on the parents and children. State why you would need to adapt your responses to children's behaviour whilst encouraging children's need for independence, control, challenge and sense of achievement. Describe how you could use these techniques during activities whilst repeating necessary exercises and how you would introduce positive reinforcement including communicating your plans and intentions to the child in an appropriate way. Why is it important to value the child and communicate t his?

....

11   Produce a leaflet for parents/carers which gives information on a range of equipment and materials for children with special needs.

    ....

14   Suggest different methods of self-evaluation.

    ....

19,25,26   Design a pack for parents who are new to your setting, include information in your pack which emphasises parents central role in their children's welfare. Discuss the nature of relationships within families and the importance of encouraging other family members to be actively involved with and accepting of a child with special needs and how constraints which living conditions may impose on parents' ability to sustain a programme.

    ....

20   Discuss how in the practical situation you will communicate with parents as equals, how to listen to parents and how to adjust and modify communication with parents according to their interest, knowledge and confidence.

    ....

22   Suggest when it is appropriate to intervene in a child's activity.

    ....

24   Discuss ways of facilitating the learning of adults.

    ....

Having completed all these portfolio activities to the required standard for the level of your award, you should present your portfolio to your assessor for assessment.

UNIT M2 MANAGE ADMISSIONS, FINANCE AND OPERATING SYSTEMS IN CARE AND EDUCATION·

Description of Knowledge, Understanding and Skills

Equipment, Materials, Environment	
1.	Methods of keeping records of income and expenditure, of children and families, of stock levels and equipment
2.	The candidate's role in relation to the policies and procedures of the setting concerning authorisation of expenditure and flexibility about families' payments
3.	Admissions policies and procedures of the setting including the candidate's role.
4.	Information required about children and families including that needed in an emergency.
5.	The requirements of the registering authority for records.
6.	The policies and procedures of the setting concerning authorisation of expenditure and ordering and hiring equipment and materials.
7.	Suitable suppliers of relevant equipment and materials including loan schemes.
8.	Suitable and safe methods of storing different types of materials.
Relationships	
9.	Information to give to parents about admissions.
10.	Boundaries and requirements for confidentiality in the setting.

UNIT M2 MANAGE ADMISSIONS, FINANCE AND OPERATING SYSTEMS IN CARE AND EDUCATION

Portfolio Activities

1 Collect and present methods of keeping records of income and expenditure, of children and families, stock levels and equipment. Blank forms are acceptable.

2 Describe your own role in relation to the policies and procedures of the setting concerning authorisation of expenditure and flexibility about families payments.

3 Describe the admission policies and procedures of your setting, plus your own involvement.

4 Compile a form that would be of use upon an admission file stating relevant information on a child/ren and their family. Include emergency contact information.

5 What are the requirements of the registering authority for records?

6.7 Describe the policies and procedures of your setting concerning authorisation of expenditure and ordering and hiring equipment and materials.

Include suitable suppliers of relevant equipment and materials including loan schemes.

8 State suitable and safe method of storing different types of materials.

9.10 What information would you give to parents about admissions? How would you describe to them the boundaries and requirements for confidentiality in the setting?

Having completed all of these portfolio activities to the required standard for the level of your award you should present your portfolio to your assessor for assessment.

UNIT M6 WORK WITH OTHER PROFESSIONALS

Description of Knowledge and Understanding Skills

Relationships	
1.	A basic knowledge of the roles of other professionals in the field of early years, care and education.
2.	A general basic knowledge of group dynamics.
3.	The aims, structure and policies of own organisation.
4.	The scope boundaries and requirements of confidentiality.
5.	The role of self in the organisation and the limitations of own competence and area of responsibility.
6.	Stereotypical assumptions, which can be undertaken, based on gender, racial origins, disability, work role and age.

UNIT M6 WORK WITH OTHER PROFESSIONALS

 Portfolio Activities

The diversity of professional staff and specialist staff working in early years care and education ensures that the best possible resources are allocated to cover the needs of all children and families. Also the purchaser and provider model of services means that many establishments involved with the care and education of children may have to negotiate contracts to provide for a set number of children, or offer guidance as a service provider.

 1,2   Compile a directory of professionals working in your local area with a section for 'Expertise' and 'Specialist Expertise'. That is appropriate to early years care and education.
The directory is for use by staff within you setting as a source of information. State how this resource can actively be used as part of a multi-disciplinary network with other professionals and with your own organisation.

....

For the following activity you will need to locate a copy of your organisation's Personal Specification or a related Description of Duties specification appropriate to employment within the early years sector. Examine the document carefully and provide evidence in relation to the following:

 3,5   Describe the stated aims and objectives of your organisation. Then provide a diagram that details the appropriate staffing structure of the organisation.

....

 4   Provide a description of the statement in relation to the Duties Specification that relates to confidentiality. How does this affect your role within the organisation?

....

6   Within your role how can you ensure that staff actively avoid stereotypical assumptions?

....

Having completed all of these portfolio activities to the required standard for the level of your award you should present your portfolio to your assessor for assessment.

UNIT M8 PLAN, IMPLEMENT AND EVALUATE ROUTINES FOR CHILDREN

Description of Knowledge, Understanding and Skills

Development		
1.	Overall course of children's development and how to meet those needs.	
2.	How routines affect children's development.	
3.	The background and previous experience of the children in the group.	
4.	Stereotypical assumptions often made in assessing children's needs and how to avoid them.	
5.	Periods of time for which children at various stages of development are capable of sustaining concentration.	
Curriculum Practice		
6.	Contingencies and variations in routine likely to occur.	
7.	How to plan and use routine activities to enhance children's learning within a given timescale.	
8.	Methods of supporting children in the development of self-help skills.	
9.	The role of routine in promoting children's security and how to recognise signs of distress and insecurity.	
10.	The need to adapt or modify planned routines to suit children's needs and interests and to capitalise on unplanned learning opportunities.	
11.	The purpose of evaluation.	
12.	How to set and use criteria for evaluation.	
13.	Methods of self evaluation.	
14.	How to analyse and assess information for implications for children's routines.	

Curriculum Practice – *continued*
15.   How to use evaluation information in future planning.
Equipment, Materials, Environment
16.   The need to take account of health and safety requirements when planning.
17.   How to make the best use of indoor and outdoor environment in implementing plans, including using seasonal variations, and the effect of the weather on the nature of activities and contingency.
18.   Facilities available in the local community.
19.   The health and safety requirements of the setting.
20.   How to use and adapt existing and readily available resources in an innovative and flexible manner.

UNIT M8 PLAN, IMPLEMENT AND EVALUATE ROUTINES IN CHILDREN

Portfolio Activities

1,2,3,4,5, 16,18,19, 20   When planning a routine for your group setting, what type of factors/ implications would you consider?

....

6,7,8,9, 10   Submit a detailed routine plan demonstrating an awareness of time scale, and the all round development of the individual children.

....

11,12,14, 15   Decide upon a set criteria for evaluation. Implement this with the daily routine. Analyse and assess the information – what does it suggest? How will this aid your future planning?

....

13   Suggest methods of self-evaluation.

....

Having completed all of these portfolio activities to the required standard for the level of your award you should present your portfolio to your assessor for assessment.

UNIT M20 INFORM AND IMPLEMENT MANAGEMENT COMMITTEE POLICIES AND PROCEDURES

Description of Knowledge, Understanding and Skills

Development	
1.	Activities and experiences to promote children's development and learning.
Curriculum Practice	
2.	The importance of varying types of activity and the way activities are presented for stimulating children's interest and enjoyment.
Equipment, Materials, Environment	
3.	Possible resources, equipment and materials available for use by the group and their potential and limitations.
4.	The nature and purpose of the report and the implications for the way information is presented.
Relationships	
5.	The roles and areas of responsibility of committee, line manager and self.
6.	The principles of meetings and the procedures adopted by the committee.
7.	The importance of providing accurate information in enabling management committees to function effectively.
8.	The reasons and benefits of operational planning.
9.	The structure, role and policies of the organisation including confidentiality.
10.	Boundaries of responsibility in relation to children in the group, parents and management committee and areas where there may be a conflict of interests.
11.	The importance of feedback and suggestions in contributing to effective policy making.
12.	The role of training in personal and professional development.

UNIT M20 INFORM AND IMPLEMENT MANAGEMENT COMMITTEE POLICIES AND PROCEDURES

Portfolio Activities

1,2   Describe appropriate activities and experience for promoting children's development and learning. State why it is important to vary the types of activities offered and their presentation.

....

3,4   List the possible resources, equipment and materials available for use by the group and their potential limitations.

....

Consider the nature and purpose of a report, comment on the implications for the way information is presented.

....

5,6,7,8, 9,10,11, 12   Devise a detailed booklet that would be used to inform a new member of staff of the roles and responsibilities of the setting committee, line manager and own role. (Include information on the listed numbered statements.)

....

Having completed all of these portfolio activities to the required standard for the level of your award you should present your portfolio to your assessor for assessment.

UNIT P4 SUPPORT PARENTS IN DEVELOPING THEIR PARENTING SKILLS

Description of Knowledge, Understanding and Skills

Development
1. Critical stages of development especially as related to commonly requested information including behaviour, toilet training, and language development, feeding social skills, effects of cultural, social and economic background on progress.
2. Range of methods and strategies in the care of children and the management of behaviour and development.

Equipment, Materials, Environment
3. Use of observation techniques to identify and record in format suitable for future reference: emotional, physical, behavioural development of a child.
4. Use of observation techniques to identify and record positive aspects of child management displayed by parents.
5. Sources of advice and information from other agencies in locality including Social Services Departments, Health Authority, Welfare Rights resources, Local Education Departments, Voluntary organisations.
6. Role of policy makers in the Local Authority, Statutory, Independent and Voluntary Sectors to ensure community resources and information about them are available to parents and providers.
7. How to identify potential barriers to access community support including physical, financial, cultural, racial and linguistic.

Relationships
8. The need and rights of children in relation to current legislation and the implications for parents and parenting.
9. Parental responsibilities and rights as expressed in relevant legislation.

Relationships – *continued*	
10.	Wide range of feelings including both positive and negative feelings parents have about their children.
11.	Indicators of positive management and provide a role model.
12.	Examples of positive interactions between parents and child.
13.	How to demonstrate positive child management and provide a role model.
14.	Understanding the use of group and individual processes for promoting parents responsibilities and positive parenting skills
15.	Awareness of the uncertainties experienced by parents in the parenting role and the low esteem and lack of skills felt by some parents.
16.	Difficulties experienced by some parents in placing their own needs in context with their child's needs and rights.
17.	Outside pressures on parents, which may affect their ability to fulfil their responsibilities to their children.
18.	Variations in family values and practise across cultural and other groupings and awareness that practices also vary within such groupings.
19.	Awareness of the significance for parents of traditional child rearing practices derived from cultural or social groupings and extended families.
20.	Difficulties experienced by some parents in acknowledging and valuing in the child all aspects of their child's racial and cultural origins.
21.	Ability to judge level of information to be communicated, content of communication and timing of communication in relation to circumstances and needs of parents.
22.	Techniques for building and valuating relationships with parents taking account of gender, race, culture and religious differences.
23.	Indicators of stereotypical patterns of parenting and different approaches, opportunities, strategies for changing stereotypical parenting practice.

UNIT P4 SUPPORT PARENTS IN DEVELOPING THEIR PARENTING SKILLS

Portfolio Activities

6.5   Research the role and function of the Portage home teaching service. Provide
1.2   a report that covers the following areas.
          The role and function of the Portage visitor to the home of parents. And the
          developmental skills they're associated with.

....

10.11   Describe the ways in which parents are actively involved with the Portage
12.13   programme and the importance of parental participation and evaluation as
15.16   part of the process.

....

3.4   Provide examples of the type of information and methods used by the Portage
          worker to identify, record and manage a child's behaviour.

....

8.9   Explain how the needs and rights of children are related to current legislation
          and the implications this has for parents. Provide and explanation for the term
          'Named Person'.

....

18.19   Discuss the implications and considerations the Portage Worker would give to
23.20   child rearing practise. Based on stereotypical parenting patterns.
22.21   What would be some of the strategies that could be used to take account of
7   cultural, religious, and gender differences. How could the worker identify
            local community support groups that would support parents?

....

14.17   Describe one voluntary organisation that supports parents experiencing
            difficulties and helps parents provide positive parenting skills.

....

*Having completed all of these portfolio activities to the required standard for the level of your award
you should present your portfolio to your assessor for assessment.*

UNIT P5 INVOLVE PARENTS IN GROUP ACTIVITIES

Description of Knowledge, Understanding and Skills

Development	
1.	A variety of methods of communication through local media and other facilities, appropriate to members of the local community and how to gain access to their use.
2.	How to present information in lively, interesting and welcoming ways.
3.	Other people or agencies able to provide information and advice.
Curriculum Practice	
4.	The nature and purpose of planned activities and events for children's development.
Relationships	
5.	The policy of the group concerning confidentiality, the importance of safeguarding confidentiality, the importance of safeguarding confidentiality of information and the boundaries of responsibility of the candidate including when and to whom requests should be referred.
6.	Awareness of the circumstances and pressures which affect parent's lives and consequently their involvement in the group, including the apprehension often felt by parents on coming into new situations, and ways of supporting them as they adjust.
7.	Awareness that values and practices differ within cultural and other groups as well as across such groups.
8.	How to communicate with parents as equals, how to listen to parents, and how to adjust and modify communication with parents, according to their interest, knowledge and confidence in the group.
9.	Information and advice commonly sought by parents.
10.	The benefits to the group, the parents and the children of parent's involvement in the group.

Relationships – *continued*	
11.	Ways of encouraging parents and carers to share experiences with each other.
12.	Different ways in which parents can participate in the group, including specific skills they may have.
13.	The variety of ways in which parents can be involved in children's activities and the importance of negotiating their type and level of involvement.
14.	The reason why some parents are reluctant to attend and participate in children's activities, what might be a barrier, real or felt by parents.
15.	How to recognise and challenge prejudice and discrimination, and how to support those who are the object of it and those who perpetrate it.
16.	Different ways of giving and receiving feedback which could assist further parental involvement including ways to make time and space available for talking with parents.

UNIT P5 INVOLVE PARENTS IN GROUP ACTIVITIES

 Portfolio Activities

> ### PARTNERSHIP WITH PARENTS
>
> There are many situations and environments in which more than one carer is involved with a child on daily basis. By involving and working with parents within the setting carers insure that parents are seen as a vital link to the caring team. This insures children can grow and develop to their full potential in all care environments. Many parents need reassurance that their child/ren will be happy and well-cared for in their absence. Therefore carers need to make children feel valued, trusted and supported in all environments.

1.2
3.9   Provide a planned programme that describes and illustrates the use of notice boards that describes in detail the information parents, and members of the local community need. You need also to provide examples of the way you would display information, that is user friendly, advertise all aspects of the setting, and provide information that is of local interest to the community.

....

12   Design a poster that could be used on your notice board that would encourages parents to use any specific skills that they have within the setting.

....

8.4
11.13
10.16   Describe how you communicate and negotiate with a group of parents who offer their skills to work within the setting. Explain how you would address the purpose of planned activities and the boundaries in which parents would be expect to work within the setting.

....

6.5   State how you would discuss any apprehension parents may feel, how you could support their efforts of involvement in ways that would foster confidence. Provide examples of how confidentiality must be respected within the setting and how this would apply to parental involvement.

....

7.15   Describe how through parental involvement you would encourage cultural diversity, and challenge any prejudicial opinions.

....

14   Explain how you would recognise and respect those parents who are reluctant to participate or be involved in the setting. Provide examples of the reasons why you feel this happens.

....

Having completed all of these portfolio activities to the required standard for the level of your award you should present your portfolio to your assessor for assessment.

UNIT P7 VISIT AND SUPPORT A FAMILY IN THEIR OWN HOME

Description of Knowledge, Understanding and Skills

Development	
1.	The significance of the bonding between parents and their children.

Equipment, Materials, Environment	
2.	The types of information likely to be needed by parents and how to communicate it effectively
3.	The involvement of other agencies with the family.
4.	Locally available support facilities and networks and how families gain access to them.
5.	Sources of information about other relevant professionals in the locality, including sources of help in cases where other languages are involved.

Relationships	
6.	The purpose of the visit and any previous arrangements made by the visiting service.
7.	The nature and underlying purpose of support offered by the visiting service.
8.	The importance of taking time to establish positive relationships with parents and the characteristics of a positive relationship.
9.	The principals of open communication and the limits and boundaries of confidentiality.
10.	How pressure of parent's circumstances can affect their communication and relationships with their children and with other adults.
11.	Awareness of possible barriers to communication and ways of overcoming them.

13.	Strategies for handling aggression and hostility include an understanding of how it arose.
14.	The rights and responsibilities of parents in relation to the home visiting situation and the need to respect them.
15.	The responsibilities of parents and the difficulties which outside pressures may put on their ability to fulfil their responsibilities.
16.	The boundaries of responsibility for work with parents and how to identify issues beyond the candidate's responsibility or competence.
17.	The reluctance of some families to share problems or the need to set boundaries to the information they wish to share.
18.	The importance of carrying out any support offered to families and not promising more than can be delivered or achieved.
19.	The policies and practices of the visiting service for sharing information about families.
20.	The circumstances in which families should be referred to senior colleagues or other professionals.

UNIT P7 VISIT AND SUPPORT A FAMILY IN THEIR OWN HOME

Portfolio Activities

6.7   Outline the role of one professional worker who is responsible for visiting a family in their own home, to offer support and provide professional advice.

....

14   State the nature of the underlining purpose for visiting the family, in relation to the service. The support the service will provide. Explain the rights and responsibilities of parents in relation to the home-visiting situation, and how you would respect the fact that this is their home.

....

1.3   Research theories relating to the significance of bonding between parent's and their children. Comment on how appropriate they are when used by agencies with the family.

....

4
5.12   Provide a list of the support facilities available to families within your local area. State the type of professionals that are available at these services, and how families gain access to them. State how you would acquire help with a family whose language and background differs from the worker.

....

8.2   Describe with examples how on your initial visit to the family you plan to establish positive relationships with the parents.

....

9.19   The type of information that parents are likely to need and how you will establish open communication with them.

....

Explain how you will clearly define the boundaries for your visit and the sharing of information about the family with other agencies. Plus the use of confidentiality in association with the policy and practice of your organisation.

....

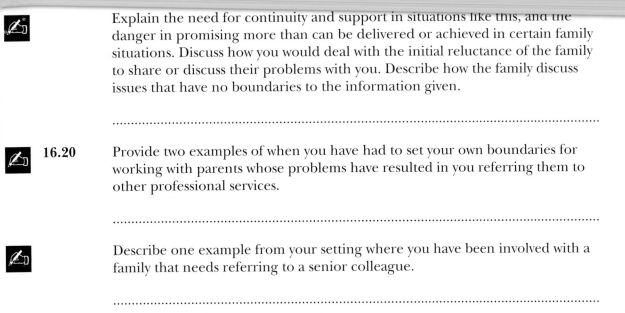

Explain the need for continuity and support in situations like this, and the danger in promising more than can be delivered or achieved in certain family situations. Discuss how you would deal with the initial reluctance of the family to share or discuss their problems with you. Describe how the family discuss issues that have no boundaries to the information given.

....

16.20   Provide two examples of when you have had to set your own boundaries for working with parents whose problems have resulted in you referring them to other professional services.

....

Describe one example from your setting where you have been involved with a family that needs referring to a senior colleague.

....

Having completed all of these portfolio activities to the required standard for the level of your award you should present your portfolio to your assessor for assessment.

UNIT P8 ESTABLISH AND MAINTAIN A CHILD CARE AND EDUCATION SERVICE

Description of Knowledge, Understanding and Skills

Development

1.	How to gather information from observation of children and parents about relationships and style of parenting.
2.	Key indicators of the sequence of child development including normal development and deviations from the normal development relative to the background of the family and the child.

Equipment, Materials, Environment

3.	The extent of the service available and the degree of flexibility within it.
4.	Other sources of information and how to evaluate its relevance for identifying the family's need.
5.	How to record information on the family's requirements.
6.	The implications of written agreements.
7.	Sources of legally tested forms of agreements.
8.	The importance of regular review of written agreements.
9.	The policy of the setting concerning confidentiality and the importance of safeguarding confidentiality of information.

Relationships

10.	The central role played by parents in children's welfare and development, and the bond between children and parents.
11.	The importance and value of parents knowledge about their children.
12.	The negative feelings some parents have about other people caring for their children.

15.	Variations in family values and practices across cultural and other groupings and awareness that practices also vary within such groups.
16.	Parents' needs for regular information about their children in order to sustain continuity of care.
17.	How to communicate with parents as equals, how to listen to parents, and how to adjust and modify communication with parents according to their interest, knowledge and confidence.

UNIT P8 ESTABLISH AND MAINTAIN A CHILD CARE AND EDUCATION SERVICE

Portfolio Activities

1 Observe the relationships between four children and their parents. Comment on their parenting skills. How did they differ? Remember confidentiality.

Could you offer any recommendations to approach situations differently?

....

2 List the key indicators of the sequence of child development. Include normal and deviations from normal development relative to the background of the family and the child.

....

3 Describe the education service that you are associated with. Comment on the degree of flexibility within it.

....

4,5,7,8 Research other sources of information and how to evaluate its relevance for identifying the family's need.

How would you record information on a family's requirements, and what would the implication be of written agreements? How often would you need to review these and why?

....

7 Comment briefly on sources of legally tested formats of agreements.

....

9 Discuss your own settings policy on confidentiality and the importance of safeguarding confidentiality of information.

You could include any policy statement that your setting has.

....

10,11,12, 13,14 Devise a booklet for parents at your setting giving detailed information upon their central role in their child's development and welfare. How they can become involved within the setting, showing awareness of family pressures and work commitments.

....

Having completed all of these portfolio activities to the required standard for the level of your award, you should present your portfolio to your assessor for assessment.

UNIT MCI C1 MANAGE YOURSELF

Element MCI. C1.1 Develop your Own Skills to Improve your Own Performance

KNOWLEDGE REQUIREMENTS

Communication

The importance of getting feedback from others on your performance and how to encourage, enable and use feedback in a constructive manner.

Management competence

The principal skills required for effective managerial performance.
The types of interpersonal skills required for effective team work.

Organisational context

The current and likely future requirements and standards within your job role and how they correspond to your level of competence as a manager.
The appropriate people from whom to get feedback on your performance.

Training and development

The importance of continuing self-development to managerial competence.

How to assess your own current level of competence.

How to develop a personal action plan for learning and self-development with realistic objectives.

The types of development activities and their relative advantages and disadvantages.

How to assess your personal progress and update your plans accordingly.

MCI. C1.2 Manage your Time to Meet your Objectives

KNOWLEDGE REQUIREMENTS

Information handling

How to assess how much information is required before an effective decision can be taken.

Planning

How to set objectives for yourself which are specific, measurable and achievable.

How to prioritise work in line with organisational objectives and policies.

How to estimate the amount of time required to carry out planned activities.

The kind of contingencies which may occur and how to assess and plan for these.

Time management

The importance of effective time management to managerial competence.
How to identify and minimise unhelpful interruptions to planned work.

Unit MCI C1 Manage Yourself

Portfolio Activity

It is essential for completion of this unit that you up-date your personal action plan regularly. You will need to liaise with your work based assessor frequently. All of your action plans should be included in your final portfolio of evidence. You must assess your own progress, obtain feedback from others on your performance and show your assessor how you have improved your performance through using this information in a constructive manner. Your action plans should include the following information: work you are aiming to complete by the next scheduled meeting with your assessor, dates and times your assessor will observe and assess your performance, meetings you need to attend with colleagues, research you need to undertake and a list of work that is complete and has been assessed by your assessor. You must demonstrate to your assessor that you can manage your time to meet your objectives. You should indicate in your action plans work that has priority, an estimation of how long you think it will take you and indicate what action you would take in the event of not being able to complete the work due to unanticipated events such as illness.

Having completed all of these portfolio activities to the required standard for the level of your award you should present your portfolio to your assessor for assessment.

UNIT MCI C4 CREATE EFFECTIVE WORKING RELATIONSHIPS

Element MCI. C4.1 Gain the Trust and Support of Colleagues and Team Members

KNOWLEDGE REQUIREMENTS

You will also need to satisfy your assessor that you know and understand:

Communication

- How to consult with colleagues in a way which encourages open and frank discussions.
- How to select communication methods appropriate to the issues and contexts.
- The importance of effective communication methods to productive working relationships.
- The importance of discussing evaluations of output and behaviour at work promptly and directly with those concerned.
- How to provide feedback in a way which will lead to a constructive outcome.

Information handling

- The types of information concerning colleagues which you need to treat confidentially and procedures to follow.

Organisational context

- The organisational plans and activities, emerging threats and opportunities, which are relevant to the work of colleagues and about which they need to be informed.

Providing support

- The support colleagues may require achieving their objectives and how to provide this support.

Working relationships

- How people work in groups.
- Strategies and styles of working which encourage effective working relationships.
- The importance of honouring commitments to colleagues.
- The importance of showing respect for colleagues and how to do this.

KNOWLEDGE REQUIREMENTS

You will also need to satisfy your assessor that you know and understand:

Communication

- The importance of keeping your manager informed of activities, progress, results and achievements and how to do this.
- How to develop and present proposals in ways which are realistic, clear and likely to influence your manager positively.

Organisational context

- The management structure, lines and accountability and control in your organisation.
- The types of emerging threats and opportunities about which your manager needs to be informed.
- The types of organisational policies and ways of working about which you need to consult with your manager and how to do this.

Working relationships

- Strategies and styles of working which encourage effective working relationships.
- Methods of handling disagreements with your manager in a constructive manner.

UNIT MCI C4 CREATE EFFECTIVE WORKING RELATIONSHIPS

Element MCI. C4.3 Minimise Conflict in your Team

KNOWLEDGE REQUIREMENTS
You will also need to satisfy your assessor that you know and understand:

Information handling

- The importance of maintaining accurate records of conflicts and their outcomes.
- The information regarding conflicts which must be treated confidentially and the people who may and may not be informed.

Organisational context

- The people to inform when conflicts are outside your area of responsibility.
- The organisational requirements regarding the handling of conflict and its resolution.

Working relationships

- Situations, behaviour and interactions between people which encourage conflict.
- How to minimise conflict between people at work.
- The importance of keeping people regularly informed of expected standards of work and behaviour.
- How to inform people of the standards and behaviour you expect of them.
- The importance of giving people opportunities to discuss problems affecting their work and how to provide such opportunities.
- How to identify potential conflict between individuals in your organisation.
- Types of conflict, which may occur between people at work and action to take in response to these, which will minimise disruption to work.

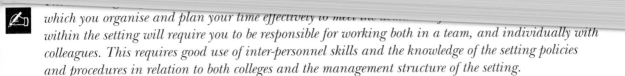

which you organise and plan your time effectively to meet the demands within the setting will require you to be responsible for working both in a team, and individually with colleagues. This requires good use of inter-personnel skills and the knowledge of the setting policies and procedures in relation to both colleges and the management structure of the setting.

To be competent in the area you will need to provide evidence that relates to working with colleagues both within a team, individually and management of the setting. Therefore your evidence can be provided from examples of documentation that relates to your own role within the setting or by supporting examples as a reflective practitioner.

You will clearly need to demonstrate that you can respond to various types of relationships with colleagues. These will need to be reflective of the variations in relationships within the setting from that of being supportive to colleagues, strategies and styles of working with colleagues that can both promote positive relationships and that of situations where different forms of conflict may occur. You will also need to consider the way in which your own role requires you to be accountable and responsible to your manager, but also the various forms of accountability with the work setting.

You may well choose to relate the setting policy and procedures for some of your evidence, but in doing so you must state how this relates to each element. Other examples can be taken from reports, extracts of appropriate minutes of meetings. Diary extracts letters to colleagues. The settings Staff Handbook, all sections will relate to various form of evidence. Clearly you must present your own evidence with examples of how you feel they relate to the knowledge evidence and demonstrate your own competency.

Having completed all of these portfolio activities to the required standard for the level of your award you should present your portfolio to your assessor for assessment.

UNIT C24 SUPPORT THE DEVELOPMENT OF CHILDREN'S LITERACY SKILLS

Description of Knowledge, Understanding and Skills

Development	
1.	Sequences and stages in the development of children's reading, writing and comprehension skills.
2.	Techniques which encourage children to read, write and comprehend.
3.	The schools policies and practices for obtaining and reporting relevant information about children's reading, writing and comprehension skills and development.
4.	Value of writing as a means of remembering, communicating, organising and developing ideas and information; and as a source of enjoyment.
Curriculum Practice	
5.	An awareness of the requirements of the National Curriculum or its equivalent to reading in English Key Stage 1 as well as other related subjects.
6.	School policies and practices and teacher requirements for supporting children's reading.
7.	Types of reading conventions that might affect reading skills and development.
8.	Types of grammatical, illustrative phonic, graphic and contextual cues and knowledge and how these can and do influence reading skills and development.
9.	Types of reading contexts, materials and sources and how they might be used to develop comprehension skill.
10.	Types of writing forms and their characteristics.
11.	Types of writing stimuli and their usefulness in the development of writing skills.

13.	The importance of spelling ~~...~~ Key Stage 1, including formation of letters of the alphabet, use of sound-symbol relationships, phonological patterns, simple spelling patterns, common prefixes and suffixes.

Equipment, Materials, Environment	
14.	The importance of selecting appropriate reading materials for children at different stages of reading development and the types of factor that may influence their choice.
15.	The effects of different settings and environment on the child's reading performance.
16.	How to enable children choose appropriate reading materials to aid their comprehension development.
17.	The effects of different settings and environments on comprehension and understanding.

UNIT C24 SUPPORT THE DEVELOPMENT OF CHILDREN'S LITERACY SKILLS

Portfolio Activities

1,2   Draw a diagram to show the sequences and stages in the development of children's reading, writing and comprehension skills. Incorporate upon this, appropriate techniques and strategies which encourage children to acquire these skills.

....

3,6   Research and present your settings policies and practises for obtaining and reporting relevant information about children's reading, writing and comprehension skills and development. Include the teacher's role for supporting children's reading.

....

4   Write a short report on the value of writing as a means of remembering, communicating, organising and developing ideas and information; and as a source of enjoyment.

....

5   This can be cross-referenced with Unit C25 point 3.

....

7   Describe the types of reading conventions that might affect reading skills and development.

....

8,9,10, 11,12   Write a detailed report on the introduction of the Literacy Hour that has been implemented in educational establishments since September 1998.

Discuss its aims and objectives for the development and enhancement of children's literacy skills, and its specific areas.

Include the yearly plan of the work to be covered by the specific year group that you work with, plus a detailed weekly plan for the hour session. State the aims and objectives of each session.

Describe a shared reading and writing session that you have implemented. What was the reaction of the children?

Did you achieve what you set out to?

....

14,15,16,17   Evaluate your classroom area for its effectiveness of promoting a literacy rich environment. Examine the reading corner, does it encourage the children to choose appropriate reading materials to their level of skill?
Make suggestions on the establishment of a good classroom practice in providing a suitable environment to promote children's comprehension and understanding. What would the effects be if this was not undertaken?

Having completed all of these portfolio activities to the required standard for the level of your award you should present your portfolio to your assessor for assessment.

UNIT C25 SUPPORT THE DEVELOPMENT OF CHILDREN'S MATHEMATICAL SKILLS

Description of Knowledge, Understanding and Skills

Development	
1.	Sequences and stages in children's mathematical development and their acquisition of mathematical concepts.
2.	Communication techniques and mathematical language which encourage children's development, understanding and use of shape, space and measure.
Curriculum Practice	
3.	Awareness of the requirements relating to Mathematics Key Stage 1 as well as other related subjects of the National Curriculum or its equivalent.
4.	School policies and practices and teacher requirements for using and applying mathematics.
5.	The importance of and activities involved in children making and monitoring decisions to solve problems at Key Stage 1 or its equivalent.
6.	The importance of and activities involved in children understanding place value, the relationships between numbers, methods of computation and solving numerical problems at Key Stage 1 or its equivalent.
7.	The importance of and activities involved in children understanding and using patterns and properties of shape position and movement and measures at Key Stage 1 or its equivalent.
8.	The types of activity appropriate for the development of mathematical language and communication development at Key Stage 1 or its equivalent.
9.	The importance of developing mathematical reasoning and the concepts and activities involved at Key Stage 1 or its equivalent.
Equipment, Materials, Environment	
10.	How to enable children to choose and use different mathematical equipment and materials.

12.	How to enable children to choose ~~...~~ recognition and calculations.
13.	Methods and materials involved in 3-dimensional and 2-dimensional modelling.
14.	How to enable children to choose and use simple measuring instruments.

Relationships	
15.	The importance of establishing an effective, confident and caring working relationship with children.
16.	The rules and boundaries of confidentiality within the setting with regard to the children's mathematical skills and development.
17.	The candidates and the teachers role in the development of mathematical concepts and applications.
18.	When it is necessary and how to access other help.

UNIT C25 SUPPORT THE DEVELOPMENT OF CHILDREN'S MATHEMATICAL SKILLS

Portfolio Activity

1,2   Design a chart to show the sequences and stages on children's mathematical development and their acquisition of mathematical concepts.
Linked to this, suggest communication techniques and mathematical language which encourage children's development, understanding and use of shape, space and measure.

....

3   Include information relating to mathematics Key Stage 1 and the other core subjects.

....

4   Produce your settings policy on maths and its practices, plus comments on the teacher requirements for using and applying mathematics.

....

5   Describe the importance of and activities involved in children making and monitoring decisions to solve problems at Key Stage 1 or its equivalent.

....

6,7   Devise and implement suitable activities that would involve children understanding the following:

- Place value
- Relationships between numbers
- Methods of computation
- Solving numerical problems
- Using patterns and properties of shape
- Position and movement and measures at Key Stage 1 or its equivalent.

....

8,9   From the above choose 2 activities and state why and how they are appropriate for the development of mathematical language and communication development. Also include the importance of developing mathematical reasoning.

....

11 Present methods ~~of~~ mathematical skills and development.

....

13 List methods and materials used in 3-dimensional and 2-dimensional modelling.

....

15 Describe why it is important to establish an effective, confident and caring working relationship with children.

....

16 State the rules and boundaries of confidentiality within the settings, with regard to the child's mathematical skills and development.

....

17,18 Discuss the teacher's and your own role in the development of mathematical concepts and applications. When do you think it would be necessary to access other help? How would you do this?

....

Having completed all of these portfolio activities to the required standard for the level of your award you should present your portfolio to your assessor for assessment.

BOOK LIST

The following books are a useful source of reference when completing the portfolio activities

M. Alcott (1998) *An Introduction to Children with Special Educational Needs.* London: Hodder & Stoughton.

T. Bruce (1998) *Early Childhood Education* 2nd Edition. London: Hodder & Stoughton.

J. Lindon (1998) *Child Protection and Early Years Work.* London: Hodder & Stoughton.

J. Lindon (1998) *Equal Opportunities in Practice.* London: Hodder & Stoughton.

V. Lyus (1998) *Management in the Early Years.* London: Hodder & Stoughton.

C. Meggitt (1999) *Caring for Babies: A Practical Guide.* London: Hodder & Stoughton.

S. Neaum and J. Tallack (1998) *Implementing the Pre-School Curriculum.* Cheltenham: Stanley Thornes.

E. and J. Sadek (1998) *Starting and Running a Nursery.* Cheltenham: Stanley Thornes.

M. Whalley (1998) *Working with Parents.* London: Hodder & Stoughton.